BROCK ENVIRONMENTAL CENTER FOR A LIVING CHESAPEAKE:
Building a Sustainable Legacy for the Bay

An Ecotone Publishing Book/2017
Copyright © 2017 by the International Living Future Institute

Ecotone Publishing — an Imprint of the International Living Future Institute

For more information write:

Ecotone Publishing
1501 East Madison Street Suite 150
Seattle, WA 98122

Author: Juliet Grable
Book Design: softfirm
Edited by: Fred McLennan

Library of Congress Control Number: 2017933778
Library of Congress Cataloging-in Publication Data

ISBN 978-0-9972368-2-8

1. ARCHITECTURE   2. ENVIRONMENT   3. PHILOSOPHY

First Edition

Printed in Canada on FSC-certified paper, processed Chlorine-Free, using vegetable-based inks.

BROCK ENVIRONMENTAL CENTER FOR A LIVING CHESAPEAKE

Building a Sustainable Legacy for the Bay

LIVING
BUILDING
CHALLENGE

TABLE OF CONTENTS

Photo: Dave Chance

FOREWORD

The Chesapeake Bay, home to the Brock Environmental Center, is a national treasure. The productivity of its waters is legendary, leading H.L. Mencken to describe it as "an immense protein factory." While pollution, habitat loss, and overfishing have taken a deadly toll over many decades, the Bay is now showing impressive signs of improvement.

One critical component to our "Save the Bay" strategy is building smarter, with less impact on the land and the water. This approach has been a hallmark of the Chesapeake Bay Foundation's efforts to restore the Bay to a much healthier state through a vigorous, planned, and committed process of regeneration.

The Chesapeake Bay Foundation's Brock Environmental Center in Virginia Beach, Virginia is aesthetically a really beautiful building that has virtually no environmental footprint. It is the culmination of more than forty-six years of eco-friendly design and construction. In 1972, the CBF built our first environmental education center near Annapolis, Maryland. This simple, one-room log cabin was built with locally sourced logs and constructed without any power tools. It had no lights or running water. A year later, we added a waterless composting toilet that, over time, decomposes human waste, converting it into useful compost.

Admittedly, that first center was more demonstration than practical application. We have come a long way since then. In 2000, CBF opened The Phillip Merrill Environmental Center, our headquarters in Annapolis. This record-setting building was the first LEED Platinum building in the world, and it has become an important visitor destination. The Merrill Center has won more than two-dozen awards, and last year it was named one of only 52 game-changing buildings in the world in the last 170 years. More than 350,000 people have visited this exceptional building and have learned how many of the building's green components can work well in their own businesses and homes.

Our next major project was the construction of the Brock Environmental Center, which was completed in 2015. It too is LEED Platinum, and it has been awarded Living Building Challenge full petal certification by the International Living Future Institute. To date, the Brock Center is one of only eleven projects to have earned this certification, and it is the first commercial building in the United States to be permitted to treat rainwater for drinking. Like the Merrill Center, the Brock Center has become a favored destination, welcoming more than 50,000 visitors in its first twenty-four months of occupancy.

2

The Brock Environmental Center is cutting edge. Wind turbines and solar panels generate more energy than we use; greywater gardens filter rain and wastewater; energy efficient windows optimize sunlight and naturally ventilate the building; geothermal wells draw on the earth's constant 56-degree temperature to provide clean, energy efficient natural heating and cooling; and LED and linear fluorescent lighting sip energy. Each of these features provides teachable moments for those who use and visit the building, and for those who experience it in this expertly researched and written work by Juliet Grable.

The Brock Center shows the world what is possible. It is just one example of how we can save The Chesapeake Bay and begin to change the world for the better. The Brock Center proves that we can build our homes, our schools, our houses of worship, and our office buildings in such a way as to have a net positive impact on the environment. And we can do this without any sacrifice to comfort, beauty, and the services we expect from our buildings.

I would be remiss if I did not acknowledge the extraordinary contributions of the team members who designed and built the Brock Environmental Center. First, Macon and Joan Brock, Jane Batten, Harry and Calvert Lester, and the entire Hampton Roads Advisory Group were all central to its success. Without their vision and profound generosity, the Brock Center would not exist. The SmithGroupJJR architectural and engineering firm, contractor Hourigan Construction, and owner's representative Skanska USA brought our vision to reality. The inspiration and vision provided by the International Living Future Institute —and especially, Jason F. McLennan—expanded our thinking of what was possible. Finally, Mary Tod Winchester and Paul Willey made it all happen. Mary Tod, our Vice President for Administration, inspired the team to raise the sustainable bar ever higher. Paul, our Director of Operations and Brock Center Project Director, spent many months away from home, guiding and overseeing the construction of the Center. He knows and loves every inch of the site and the structure.

To Juliet Grable, thank you for telling this story of the Brock Environmental Center.

WILLIAM C. BAKER
PRESIDENT, CHESAPEAKE BAY FOUNDATION

ACKNOWLEDGEMENTS

I am honored to have been given the opportunity to tell the story of the Brock Environmental Center. This project, so much bigger than the sum of its parts, could not have happened without the contributions of many people, and I have been truly humbled by the passion, dedication, and positive energy surrounding its creation.

So too, this book could not have happened without the contributions of many. Whether core members of the design and construction team, Chesapeake Bay Foundation staff, or invested community members, people generously shared their time with me so that the story of the Brock Center might accurately reflect the richness and depth of the experience. Special thanks to Billy Almond, Will Baker, Jane Batten, Chris Brandt, Macon Brock, Dafeng Cai, Brian Coffield, Cindy Cogil, Christy Everett, Chuck Foster, Barry Frankenfield, Lynda Frost, Chris Gorri, Janet Harrison, Elizabeth Heider, Sara Lappano, Harry Lester, Greg Mella, Rich Moore, Megan O'Connell, Rus Perry, Tyler Park, Brian Solis, Walter Weeks, Paul Willey, Neil Williams, Kate Wilson, and Mary Tod Winchester. As this list cannot represent everyone who participated in this ground-breaking project, I would also like to acknowledge everyone else who contributed time, knowledge, and enthusiasm to the Brock Center.

I would like to especially thank Greg Mella of SmithGroupJJR for being the ideal client. His humor, intelligence and professionalism, along with his obvious passion for the project, made every conversation a pleasure. I would also like to acknowledge Chris Gorri and Janet Harrison, who cheerfully and promptly answered countless emailed questions.

I would like to express my gratitude to CBF staff, especially Chris Gorri and Mary Tod Winchester, who so graciously welcomed me to the Brock Center and immediately made me feel like a part of the Brock family.

I would like to thank Michael Berrisford of Ecotone Publishing, whose firm but gentle hand guided this project to successful completion, Fred McLennan for his editorial excellence, and Erin Gehle and Johanna Björk of softfirm, whose artistic design and layout so perfectly reflects the spirit of the Brock Environmental Center.

Thank you, Jason F. McLennan, Amanda Sturgeon, and everyone else at the International Living Future Institute for providing an uncompromising vision of where we need to go.

The mission of the Chesapeake Bay Foundation dovetails beautifully with the goals of the Living Building Challenge. I would like to acknowledge CBF staff and the thousands of people who are working toward the restoration of the Chesapeake Bay, especially the educators who are teaching the next generation to care for their world.

Finally, I would like to thank my husband, Brint Borgilt. In this project, as in many others, I often leaned on his intelligence, artistic eye, and experience as a builder and residential designer.

AUTHOR PROFILE

JULIET GRABLE

Juliet Grable is a freelance writer and editor whose work covers a range of topics related to sustainability. Juliet is the author of another Living Building Challenge Series book, *Desert Rain House: Resilient Building, Sustainable Living in the High Desert*, that chronicles the design and construction of the first residential project in the world to be fully certified as a Living Building. Juliet has served as Managing Editor for *Green Builder* Magazine; she still contributes to that publication and many others, including *Earth Island Journal* and *Home Power* Magazine. In addition to stories about regenerative design and construction, her writing covers innovative water systems, watershed restoration, and trends in electric vehicles and renewable energy systems. Juliet is grateful to live in Oregon's Southern Cascades with her husband Brint and cats Henri and Pico.

5

PART I

An Urgent Mission

Catalyst for a Living Chesapeake

7

Part I: **AN URGENT MISSION**

The Brock Environmental Center is deeply connected to The Chesapeake Bay.
Photo: Prakash Patel

BROCK ENVIRONMENTAL CENTER FOR A LIVING CHESAPEAKE

"There is but one entrance by sea into this country, and that is at the mouth of a very goodly bay, 18 or 20 miles broad. The land, white hilly sands like unto the Downs, and all along the shores rest plenty of pines and firs... Within is a country that may have the prerogative over the most pleasant places known, for large and pleasant navigable rivers, heaven and earth never agreed better to frame a place for man's habitation."

CAPTAIN JOHN SMITH

THE BROCK ENVIRONMENTAL CENTER: AN INTRODUCTION

To reach the Chesapeake Bay Foundation's Brock Environmental Center, you must walk along a winding footpath through a maritime forest of loblolly pines and live oaks. At the edge of the forest, the path guides you through an arch made from local driftwood, and the view opens up. For a moment, the arch frames the building. An inviting ramp leads the eye to the graceful curves of a roof that appears to be clad in silver scales. The sound of children's voices may waft up from the pavilion underneath. If there is a breeze, you can hear the whirring blades of the two wind turbines which bookend the building.

The Brock Environmental Center is an educational building, housing the staff and programs that help CBF carry out its mission. However, the center also welcomes visitors of all varieties, from students learning about the ecology of the creeks to volunteers restoring oyster habitat to individuals stealing a peaceful moment away from work. A covered deck flanking the back of the building invites people to linger and contemplate the water; a light-filled hallway connecting staff offices and the larger common areas preserve the views of the marshes and Lynnhaven River all along its length.

You never forget where you are.

As a Living Building, the Brock Environmental Center aspires to go far beyond simply creating no negative impact; it seeks to actively restore its surroundings, just as the activities CBF holds at the site contribute to the restoration and understanding of The Chesapeake Bay.

Through these complementary missions, the Brock Environmental Center is a conduit for a cleaner bay, healthier ecosystems, and thriving plant, animal, and human communities —a catalyst for a Living Chesapeake.

AN ESTUARY IN TROUBLE

The Chesapeake Bay is the largest estuary in the United States. The Chesapeake Bay watershed encompasses 64,000 square miles and includes parts of six states and the District of Columbia.

When John Smith and his crew first explored and mapped the Bay in 1607, they found a thriving, diverse ecosystem. Up to 50,000 Native American people representing at least three language families lived in settlements along the many rivers that feed into the Bay. These peoples cultivated land, clearing patches of forest so they could grow beans, squash, corn and tobacco. They hunted deer and other game in the maritime forests. They fished. They harvested clams, mussels and oysters. And though their activities did impact the land, their numbers were small, and their semi-nomadic lifestyles ensured that lands depleted by farming could eventually recover.

Jamestown, established in Virginia in 1608, became the first permanent English colony, largely thanks to support from the native Powhatan Indians. This colony ushered in a wave of British settlement. Though their numbers were small at first, the impact was immediate. Native human populations felt it first. War and especially disease literally decimated their numbers, so that by the 1650s, just 2,400 indigenous peoples remained.

The new settlers cleared forests and drained marshes to create buildable and farmable land. At the time of the American Revolution, 700,000 colonists were living in the watershed. Pennsylvania established itself as a major dairying and farming state. Cities such as Baltimore, Annapolis, and Washington, DC sprang up along major rivers. Sewage and industrial effluent from these burgeoning urban centers was routed into the rivers that fed The Chesapeake Bay.

The oyster became a staple of The Chesapeake Bay region's economy. Advances in refrigeration and transportation in the mid-nineteenth century allowed Chesapeake Bay oysters to be shipped all across the country by rail. Watermen mined the mollusks from the Bay, venturing further from inland shores as the reefs were depleted—activity which also destroyed critical habitat. Canneries sprang up along the shores, and clam, blue crab, and rockfish fisheries thrived.

By the turn of the twentieth century, three million people were living in The Chesapeake Bay watershed, and 70 percent of the forests had been cleared—first for house and boat building, then for charcoal and agriculture, and finally, to make way for development. The stripped forests along with tillage agriculture sped up erosion and sent large volumes of sediment downriver. The advent of commercial fertilizers added nitrogen and phosphorus loads to the Bay, advancing eutrophication.

Population growth accelerated through the latter part of the 20th century. The number of people living in The Chesapeake Bay watershed more than doubled from 1950 to 2014, to 18 million.

Estuaries are resilient ecosystems, but by the mid-1980s, The Chesapeake Bay could no longer absorb the many pressures associated with uncontrolled population growth, intensive agriculture, and urban development.

"Think of a vicious cycle," explains Chesapeake Bay Foundation president Will Baker. "Too much pollution degrading the Bay's water quality. Overharvesting of critical species like oysters, crabs, and rockfish. Destroying forests, wetlands, underwater grasses, and even oyster reefs—natural filters that once were nature's way of protecting the Bay. Each of these problems exacerbated the others. Ultimately, the whole of the problem was greater than the sum of its parts—a Bay system dangerously out of balance. Each of us paid the price."

Excess nutrients flowing into the Bay from the major rivers fed algae blooms, which gobbled up oxygen, creating "dead zones" in The Chesapeake Bay that formed each summer and persisted into fall. Fisheries suffered. Degraded water quality, habitat loss, disease and overharvesting pushed the oyster, the iconic species that for many defined The Chesapeake Bay, to the verge of collapse.

"When I was a child, I saw a bumper sticker that changed my life. It read 'Save the Bay.' I believe those same three little words could change the world."

WILL BAKER
Chesapeake Bay Foundation

A sign of excess nitrogen and phosphorus loading, algae blooms become visible in The Chesapeake Bay during the summer months.
Photo: Wolfgang Vogelbein, Virginia Institute of Marine Science

"The Chesapeake Bay is a single system draining and connecting six states, the District of Columbia, more than 18 million people, and thousands of species of wildlife. In our 50-year history, CBF has been fortunate to develop a robust set of tools and strategies to achieve our mission of a saved Bay. We educate, advocate, restore, and, when all else fails, litigate to put the Chesapeake back in balance. We see a triple bottom line in saving the Bay—an improved environment; fewer risks to human health; and a healthier, more robust economy."

WILL BAKER
Chesapeake Bay Foundation

"Several key people have thirty-plus years with CBF, and they still have the same strong conviction that we're going to save the Bay. We're a very passionate organization."

PAUL WILLEY
Chesapeake Bay Foundation

Photo: Garth Lenz

Photo: Kayla Deur

INFLUENCING SCHOOL CURRICULA

One pillar of The Chesapeake Bay Foundation's mission is outdoor environmental education: helping people make the connection between their everyday actions and the Bay's water quality.

Programs throughout the school year introduce thousands of students to The Chesapeake Bay and the principles of ecology. In summer, CBF hosts a teacher training institute consisting of over 30 one-week workshops. At the institute, teachers develop tools they can take back to the classroom, ensuring that the students' field experience is one component of a comprehensive environmental education course.

"We start in their 'backyards,' then work our way downstream to the Chesapeake and a local community," says Paul Willey, Director of Education Operations for CBF. "We connect their choices at home with local and downstream consequences, good or bad." Many of the teachers have

been bringing groups of students to fall or spring programs for thirty years. School principals and even superintendents attend programs, as well.

"CBF's environmental education program may be the largest in the country. Not only do we provide field education experience; we also advocate for environmental literacy and systemic environmental education throughout the region," says CBF President Will Baker. "Our program is broadly recognized as a model and the greatest long-term investment in saving the Bay that we could make."

One of CBF's greatest accomplishments is seen in Maryland, which has mandated an environmental literacy requirement for high school graduates. CBF worked with Maryland's nine largest counties to pilot the program, and it has now been implemented across the state. CBF is working on a similar initiative in Virginia and is looking ahead to Pennsylvania.

Residential and day-long field programs introduce thousands of kids to The Chesapeake Bay every year. Photo: Kayla Deur

A COORDINATED EFFORT TO SAVE THE BAY

In 1966, a group of citizens approached the governor of Maryland to do something about the dying bay.

"The governor said citizens messed it up; citizens need to fix it, and we'll help," says Mary Tod Winchester, who joined the young Chesapeake Bay Foundation as a volunteer in 1971. Today, she serves as Vice President of Administration for the organization.

CBF's mission has remained the same in the 50 years since its founding: to act as a citizen lobby for The Chesapeake Bay, to provide environmental education, and to use litigation to effect changes in policy. Since the 1980s, CBF has expanded into proactive restoration, rehabilitating and reestablishing wetlands, underwater grasses and oyster reefs.

CBF was the first organization to successfully argue that the National Environmental Policy Act, or NEPA, applies to all federal actions, not just federal environmental agencies. In the last ten to fifteen years, the organization's litigation efforts have become more strategic and proactive, with a team of litigators organized under a vice president.

Today, CBF's staff has grown to 200, with headquarters in Annapolis, Maryland and regional offices in Pennsylvania, Virginia, and Washington, DC. The organization operates educational facilities and farms throughout the watershed. Through both residential and day programs, CBF exposes 40,000 people to the Bay's wetlands, rivers and streams each year. For many, it is their first time out on the water.

"At the heart of our work is education—getting the kids out, getting them muddy and inspired so they want to make a difference," says Christy Everett, CBF's Hampton Roads Director.

For decades, CBF and a myriad of national, regional, state and local organizations have worked to reverse the vicious cycle of negative impacts. Updated wastewater treatment plants and

14

Hands-on education is one of CBF's key missions.

Part I: AN URGENT MISSION

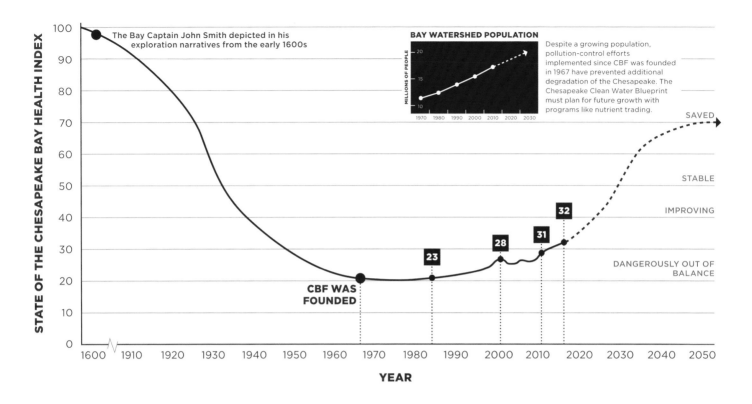

The Bay Captain John Smith depicted in his exploration narratives from the early 1600s

BAY WATERSHED POPULATION

Despite a growing population, pollution-control efforts implemented since CBF was founded in 1967 have prevented additional degradation of the Chesapeake. The Chesapeake Clean Water Blueprint must plan for future growth with programs like nutrient trading.

SAVED

STABLE

IMPROVING

DANGEROUSLY OUT OF BALANCE

CBF WAS FOUNDED

23 28 31 32

STATE OF THE CHESAPEAKE BAY HEALTH INDEX

YEAR

improved agricultural practices have reduced the burden of pollution flowing into the Bay; at the same time, restoration of forestland, wetlands, underwater grasses and oyster reefs have returned natural buffers and filters to the ecosystem.

In 1998, CBF began publishing a biennial "State of the Bay" report, which ranks The Chesapeake Bay's health according to thirteen indicators in three categories: pollution, habitat, and fisheries. The index measures each indicator against a theoretical pristine Bay with a "perfect" score of 100. Since the low point in the mid-1980s, several of the thirteen indicators, including oysters, have shown improvement, and the overall score is slowly trending upwards. The annual dead zone is not persisting as late into fall, and this trend is strong enough to discount the annual fluctuations caused by changing weather patterns.

Huge challenges remain. In 2014, the Bay's score was 32, keeping it in the "Dangerously out of Balance" category. Agriculture still contributes the most pollution to The Chesapeake Bay, yet most programs for limiting such pollution are voluntary. Cities keep growing, and with more development comes the increased burden

of stormwater pollution, which is one of the most expensive pollution sources to control. Meanwhile, fisheries are constantly pushing to raise catch quotas, threatening the modest recoveries.

The EPA declared The Chesapeake Bay an Impaired Water Body under the Clean Water Act in 1998, and called for the establishment of a Total Maximum Daily Load for the Bay. This sets a daily limit on the amount of nitrogen, phosphorus and sediment pollution that can enter the Bay. In 2010, The Chesapeake Bay received a huge boost with the implementation of the Clean Water Blueprint, a comprehensive plan developed by the six Chesapeake Bay states in cooperation with the federal government to meet these thresholds.

In the latest State of the Bay report, released in January of 2017, the overall score jumped two points to a new high of 34 (C-)—clearly reinforcing the hope that the Bay is, in fact, improving.

"Many scientists believe the Bay may be near a tipping point for the good," says Baker. "We may see a saved Bay in our lifetimes."

THE NATIVE OYSTER: A STUDY IN RESILIENCE

At one time, oyster reefs defined the major river channels and fringed the marshes of The Chesapeake Bay. Oysters are filter feeders; a single oyster can process fifty gallons of water a day, consuming small organic particles and naturally clarifying the water. Oysters share a beneficial existence with underwater grasses, and the reef structure creates nursery habitat for young fish and other creatures.

Unfortunately, a combination of impacts has devastated oyster populations. By the 1880s, 50,000 "oystermen" were working the waters of The Chesapeake Bay; by 1920, dredging operations had destroyed three-quarters of the Bay's oyster reefs. Sediment smothered many of those that remained. Pollution compromised the oysters, likely making them more vulnerable to disease parasites such as MSX and Dermo, which began affecting populations in the 1950s. By the late twentieth century, harvests had fallen to less than 1 percent of historic levels.

CBF and other organizations successfully fought an effort to introduce non-native oysters, which are less vulnerable to diseases and compromised water quality. Instead, research and restoration efforts focused on saving the native oyster. Improvements in agriculture, wastewater treatment and stormwater management began to reduce the pollution load. More and larger sanctuaries were established, where harvesting is not allowed, and CBF and other organizations actively restored reefs. Hardier, disease-resistant oysters also emerged.

Aquaculture was legalized in every county in Maryland in 2009, and both Maryland and Virginia have encouraged and invested in the industry. Private oyster operations have added millions of oysters to the Bay, while boosting the economies of both states.

Thanks to all of these efforts and many partnerships, the native oyster has begun to rebound. In 2015, for the first time in thirty years, over one million bushels of oysters were harvested. Of these, half were wild; half were the products of aquaculture. The "farmed" oysters do not form reefs, but they filter water and improve water quality just as their wild counterparts do.

Jackie Shannon and Heather North lead CBF's comprehensive restoration program in Virginia, overseeing an army of volunteers who rebuild reefs and "seed" them with juvenile native oysters. They also manage a recycling program to collect oyster shells from area restaurants, which are then used to rebuild reefs. Individuals can also participate in CBF's oyster gardening program, through which they learn first-hand about the invaluable ecosystem services oysters provide.

"Citizens who grow oysters through our oyster gardening program contribute live oysters and habitat to the Bay," says Christy Everett, CBF's Hampton Roads director. "This activity helps them become more aware and engaged in pollution reduction efforts."

A robust restoration program is helping the native oyster regain its important role in The Chesapeake Bay ecosystem.
Photos: CBF and Laura Engelund

A LEGACY OF GREEN BUILDINGS

CBF's commitment to green building is as old as the organization. For CBF, teaching people how to live in a way that minimizes negative impacts to the environment is as important as educating them about The Chesapeake Bay ecosystems.

The Foundation has built or renovated several buildings which serve as environmental education centers and demonstration buildings for the many children and teachers who attend CBF's programs. These are often located in relatively pristine areas with sensitive habitats, such as on islands or at the edge of marshes. The Fox Island Environmental Education Center was one of the first. CBF remodeled an existing hunting and fishing lodge, which was built in 1929, and began using it for residential "immersion programs" for middle and high schoolers.

"The first thing they did was remove the generator," says Janet Harrison, architect and green consultant who has worked with CBF on various projects since the 1970s.

Fox Island is completely off the grid; it relies on a solar PV array, bicycle-powered well pump, and Clivus Multrum composting toilets. A wood stove and operable windows provide natural heating and cooling.

Other buildings followed, including the Karen Noonan Environmental Center, located on twenty acres of marsh in south Dorchester County, Maryland, and the Port Isobel Environmental

Located on Fox Island, which is surrounded by Tangier and Pocomoke Sounds, the Fox Island Environmental Education Center was CBF's first foray into sustainable building. Photo: Dave Hartcorn

Education Center, located on Port Isobel Island in Virginia. These buildings utilize composting toilets and also incorporate recycled materials and natural ventilation.

"On each building, our thinking evolved," says Harrison. "It was a wonderful laboratory. We learned what worked and what didn't, and which features resonated with the kids."

In order to fully take advantage of the buildings as teaching tools, CBF showcased as many green features as possible. For example, holes were left in the interior walls of the Karen Noonan Center, so that students could see the recycled newspaper insulation.

"We never would have been able to do what we did at the Merrill Center without our other projects. Take the Clivus Multrum composting toilet. To have one of those in an office building—even for us —was a big deal. You couldn't have gone from zero to Clivus without some history."

CHUCK FOSTER
Chesapeake Bay Foundation

"LEEDING" THE WAY: THE PHILIP MERRILL ENVIRONMENTAL CENTER

In the mid-1990s, CBF was a growing organization, with four offices scattered throughout Annapolis. The Board tasked Mary Tod Winchester and CBF Chief of Staff Chuck Foster with finding a new headquarters building, so that all of the Annapolis staff could work under one roof.

After two years, the search for the right building to renovate was still on. Finally, the Bay Ridge Civic Association contacted Winchester about an intriguing property right on the edge of Annapolis, on a peninsula between the Severn and South Rivers. The thirty-three acres included a beach, a community swimming pool, parking, and the Bay Ridge Inn, which was used for events and weddings. The acreage also held the remnants of several ecosystems, including shoreline, tidal marshes, native grass meadows, and maritime forest.

"The property had been loved to death," says Winchester. "But we realized we could do everything that we do all over the Bay, including restoration with volunteers, there."

The community had effectively stopped efforts to develop the parcel commercially. Scuttled plans included a chain hotel and a development of fifty-one exclusive homes.

CBF bought the property in 1997 and, understanding the importance of strong community ties, immediately gave nearly three acres back to the community. The Bay Ridge Civic Association now operate a community pool at that site.

The search for an architecture firm was on. At that time, there were not many firms specializing in "green" construction. CBF narrowed their choice down to three candidates, one of which was SmithGroupJJR, a large national architecture, planning, and engineering firm with nine offices around the country and a tenth in Shanghai.

As part of the process, CBF took representatives from each firm on a boat tour of its facilities.

"We wanted them to understand who we were and what we did," says Winchester. "We'd been incorporating new ways of reducing our impact on the environment since the 1970s. This was the perfect time to be able to look at it holistically."

In response, CBF asked the firms to take them on a site visit to the building or group of buildings that best reflected the spirit of what CBF was trying to accomplish. SmithGroupJJR took Winchester, Foster, their "task force," and several CBF board members to the National Conservation Training Center, a campus of the U.S. Fish and Wildlife Service located on the Potomac River in Shepherdstown, West Virginia. The eighteen buildings were designed and built at the same time, and they draw heavily from regional vernacular architecture such as stone mills and barns. The durable and low-maintenance buildings were

An early sketch created by Donna McIntire illustrates how the Merrill Center design concept emerged. It shows the building form in section, and how it would integrate the sustainable attributes that came out of the charrette.

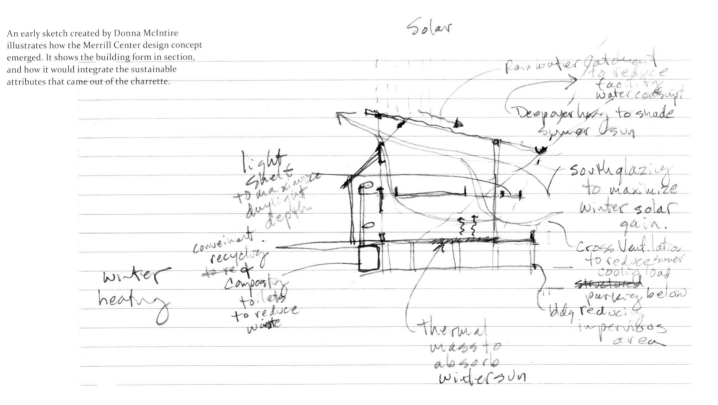

> *"The real legacy of the Merrill Center, because it was the first LEED Platinum building in the world, was the countless number of people who came to see it. It transformed how people thought about green building and expanded the realm of what was possible."*
>
> **GREG MELLA**
> SmithGroupJJR

SmithGroupJJR took a holistic approach when designing the National Conservation Training Center in West Virginia.

oriented for passive solar heating in winter, and the placement of windows, shading devices and overhangs prevents unwanted solar gain in summer and facilitates cooling without electricity. The campus also includes its own wastewater treatment plant, which incorporates constructed wetlands. The holistic design approach and aesthetic resonated strongly with the CBF team, and SmithGroupJJR was awarded the contract.

"One of the real selling points, aside from their enthusiasm, was the integration," says Foster. "They had everything but landscaping and civil engineering in-house." Donna McIntire served as project manager for the project; a young architect named Greg Mella was brought on at the end of schematic design. Don Posson led the engineering team, and a young engineer named Cindy Cogil was brought on at the same time as Mella. The architects and engineers worked closely together to create an integrated, high-performance design.

Early on, SmithGroupJJR assembled a group of industry leaders, including Greg Franta and Bill Reed, to meet at the site for a design charrette.

"The team really got to know the CBF," says Mella. "It was unusual to have that much collaboration with the owner."

CBF hired Janet Harrison as green consultant for the project. She began researching green building certification programs, including a very new program called Leadership in Energy and Environmental Design, or LEED, which was developed by the U.S. Green Building Council.

"One of the directives we had from the CBF Board was that, if we were going to build a green building, we had to get recognition for it," says Foster.

Rather than creating an initial design and applying sustainability features to it after the fact, the charrette yielded a list of desirable features that drove the design. These included rainwater collection, renewable energy in the form of a solar photovoltaic array, natural daylighting, and the use of porches for both natural ventilation and to prevent unwanted solar heat gain in summer. CBF also wanted to incorporate as many renewable materials as possible and, of course, to include composting toilets.

21

The Merrill Center includes a bris-soleil to protect the building from unwanted solar heat gain.

"The design process between CBF and our team was extremely collaborative. CBF came to the table with twenty-five years of experience in green buildings; they knew what worked and what didn't. They suggested strategies that we might have been too shy to suggest— for example, using composting toilets."

GREG MELLA
SmithGroupJJR

"CBF really is a special breed. People pursue LEED for different reasons. CBF did it because it aligned with their mission. They were living and breathing sustainability before anyone heard of sustainability."

CINDY COGIL
SmithGroupJJR

"The girls are a riot. When they first go into the bathroom and see the composting toilets, their first reaction is 'Eww!' But then they come rushing out to their friends, saying 'come look at this!'"

MARY TOD WINCHESTER
Chesapeake Bay Foundation

22

GREEN FEATURES

The building was completed in 2001 and christened the Philip Merrill Environmental Center, in honor of philanthropist Philip Merrill, who donated $7 million to the project. It was the first certified LEED Platinum building in the world, and it immediately became an iconic green building.

The Merrill Center consists of two buildings connected by a breezeway. The 32,000 square-foot facility houses a staff of approximately 100 people, and it can accommodate education programs and conferences simultaneously. Access to water, wetlands, and creeks makes it an ideal spot for hands-on programs.

LEED was unique in that it was the first major green building program to define a broader understanding of sustainability, beyond energy efficiency. The Merrill Center project anticipated many of the concerns that have guided green building certification programs since, including later iterations of LEED and the Living Building Challenge. The holistic approach to the project considered all aspects of sustainability, from responsible materials selection to the health and well-being of building occupants. Here is an overview of the Merrill Center's sustainable features:

SITE: The Merrill Center was built on the footprint of the old swimming pool, over the most disturbed portion of the property. The rest of the site was left undisturbed or enhanced through restoration. Xeriscaping with native vegetation reduced water consumption. The building was elevated to protect it against storm surges; this design decision also enabled one third of the required parking to be located underneath the building— a strategy which also reduced site disturbance.

WATER: Consistent with its mission of saving the Bay, CBF paid close attention to water conservation and the building's impact on water quality. Collected rainwater is used for handwashing as well as all non-potable uses. The original design called for using treated rainwater exclusively, but after granting initial approval for the system, the Maryland Department of Health ultimately only allowed treated rainwater for non-potable uses. Still, the rainwater system combined with the composting toilets cuts potable water use by over 90 percent, when compared to a similar commercial building. Stormwater management strategies include rain gardens, infiltration basins, and the use of permeable materials for parking areas.

ENERGY: A number of strategies work together to reduce energy use. An envelope constructed with structural insulated panels (SIPs) reduces thermal bridging and air leakage. The buildings are sited to take advantage of cooling breezes; operable windows and the building's form facilitate stack and cross-ventilation. South-facing glazing maximizes solar gain in winter, while a bris-soleil prevents solar heat gain during summer months. Geothermal wells take advantage of the constant temperature of the earth to preheat and precool air for space heating and cooling. Natural daylighting cuts the need for artificial lighting, and occupancy sensors reduce "wasted" lighting when rooms are not occupied. Finally, renewable energy systems, including a solar thermal system for water heating and a small solar PV array, offset energy use from non-renewable sources.

MATERIALS: Material conservation began with the existing buildings, which were deconstructed and the materials salvaged. The remaining concrete foundations were chipped and used as fill underneath the new entry road and parking area. The Merrill Center incorporates durable, earth-based materials such as metal for siding and roofing and wood for the envelope, cabinetry and flooring. Rapidly renewable materials, including parallel-strand engineered timbers, cork and bamboo, were used wherever

23

possible; recycled pickle barrels were made into exterior louvers to shade windows. In addition, many of the materials were left unfinished, cutting both costs and material use.

FLEXIBILITY AND ACCESSIBILITY: CBF opted for an open plan for staff offices, which not only reduced the overall building size, but ensures all of the occupants enjoy the advantages of natural daylighting and ventilation. The space can be reconfigured as the organization grows or changes, without requiring the building to physically expand.

HEALTH AND INDOOR AIR QUALITY: Use of low-VOC products and non-toxic materials contribute to the building's indoor air quality, as does increased ventilation and the use of natural ventilation via operable windows. Fresh air and ample natural daylighting contribute to the well-being of staff.

TRANSPARENCY AND EDUCATION: CBF regards the entire building as a teaching tool. Part of the impetus for leaving structures such as SIPs exposed on the inside and putting other features like rainwater cisterns in highly visible locations was to educate staff and visitors alike about the Merrill Center's sustainable technologies.

Perhaps most importantly, the Merrill Center works for the client.

"It's an excellent, functioning building for CBF and its mission," says Foster. "We made sure we designed a building and selected a property where everything CBF does—education, restoration, and advocacy—can all be here and work."

The Philip Merrill Center showcases technologies such as rainwater collection in highly visible locations, so they can function as teaching tools.

Access to several habitat types makes the Merrill Center site an ideal setting for environmental education. Photo: Nikki Davis

THE MERRILL CENTER'S LEGACY

The Merrill Center has evolved in the years since it was commissioned. Tweaks have improved energy efficiency and, in some cases, addressed issues that were not anticipated. The lessons learned through this landmark project would prove invaluable when CBF embarked on its next building project, more than a decade later.

Even before construction was completed, the Merrill Center was attracting attention. So many people requested formal visits that Winchester created a program of regularly scheduled tours. An estimated 350,000 visitors have come to the Merrill Center since the building was commissioned.

"We really focused on the people whose minds we needed to change or enlighten: architecture schools, architecture firms, and contractors, but also decision makers and owners, particularly business owners," says Winchester. Unexpectedly, the Merrill Center also became a desirable venue for weddings and conferences.

"We didn't design the building to host weddings, but we've found that these kinds of events bring in people who typically wouldn't come here," says Winchester. "And if you can make that kind of connection, then they go out and tell others."

The Merrill Center earned the Good Design is Good Business Award from BusinessWeek/Architectural Record in 2001—the first time a "green" project was recognized for the award. In 2001, the Merrill Center won the prestigious AIA COTE Top Ten Award. It has continued to garner awards in the time since, including the Center for the Built Environment's Livable Building Award in 2008; more recently, *ARCHITECT* Magazine recognized the Merrill Center as one of the Top Five green buildings constructed since 1980.

Mella and Cogil of SmithGroupJJR found themselves thrust into the role of the project's spokespersons. The project launched Mella's career as an architect specializing in sustainable design, and Cogil's as an engineer focused on progressive sustainable educational buildings.

SmithGroupJJR stayed connected with CBF and the building in the years that followed, documenting operational energy-use data, gathering lessons learned on what worked and what didn't, and helping CBF to earn Energy Star certifications. Although unusual, this continued involvement reflected CBF's approach to its buildings as living laboratories and teaching tools.

25

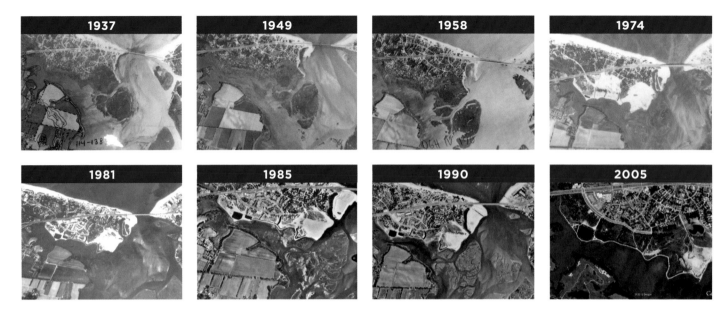

Over a period of decades, diking and the dumping of dredge spoils dramatically altered the topography and shoreline of Pleasure House Point.

A NEW ENVIRONMENTAL CENTER ON PLEASURE HOUSE POINT

Meanwhile, CBF continued to grow. One of its offices was in Norfolk, Virginia, in an area known as Tidewater to locals and Hampton Roads to everyone else.

This region, located at the south end of The Chesapeake Bay, encompasses southeast Virginia and northeast North Carolina and includes several large municipalities. Virginia Beach is the largest of these, although the region is probably best known for the Norfolk Naval base, the largest naval base in the world.

It is a region with a rich maritime history, characterized by the complex network of waterways draining into The Chesapeake Bay proper. In fact, Hampton Roads refers to the "roadstead," or shipping channels leading into the harbor.

Despite its presence in Norfolk, CBF's leadership recognized that the organization was not realizing its potential in this region. A "mobile boat" program had been operating in the area for years. The boat traveled from place to place, hosting educational programs for youth on board. But there was no land-based program.

"Most people we worked with never came to our office, and we never saw our educators," says Christy Everett. "Elected officials never saw us educating students."

In the mid-2000s, Everett and then CBF Director of Facilities Paul Willey were charged with locating a property—a place where the organization could host education programs and volunteers who wanted to help save the Bay.

They spent five years looking before settling on leasing a parcel owned by the City of Virginia Beach. It was perched just south of the mouth of The Chesapeake Bay, right next to the Lynnhaven Inlet, and had many of the characteristics CBF was looking for. But there was another, more intriguing property just on the other side of the inlet, on a protrusion of land called Pleasure House Point. This privately-owned parcel included a mile of waterfront and nearly one hundred twenty acres of wetlands, coastal dunes and maritime forest.

2012

Pleasure House Point was by no means pristine. Starting in the 1950s, the Army Corps of Engineers began dumping dredge spoils on the site. Between 1971 and 1972, over 1 million cubic yards were placed atop what was mostly wetlands. The wind shaped this material into dunes, which the Corps flattened in order to tame the blowing sands, raising the level by four to five feet in some places. A dike and a series of channels were built to contain the material and prevent it from polluting the river with sediment. By the mid-1980s, the land started to recover; by the 2000s, it was largely revegetated, and breaches in the dike had reintroduced some of the wetlands to tidal influence.

Despite the fact that Pleasure House Point had been privately owned for decades, the neighboring Ocean Park community regarded it as public space and used it for fishing and boating access. A network of walking paths and ATV trails snaked through the sand. Unfortunately, some people also used the site as a dumping ground.

In 2007, the land changed hands. The new owner, L.M. Sandler and Sons, released plans for Indigo Dunes, a 1,100-unit condominium development. The community blanched at the prospect, and began using every strategy possible to stall the project.

The City of Virginia Beach had also been eying the property, hoping to add some or all of it to its inventory of Open Space land.

"We were looking across the inlet at Pleasure House Point, wondering 'what if,' then went back to our meeting with the city to talk about the lease," recalls Willey. "At the end of the meeting, we mentioned Pleasure House Point. It was as if they were waiting for us to ask."

Everett and Willey reported back to CBF about the Pleasure House Point property, emphasizing that it was likely a long shot. CBF President Will Baker was unfazed. "Think big; why not?" he directed Everett in an email.

27

THE PURCHASE OF PLEASURE HOUSE POINT

City of Virginia Beach:
Open Space Fund
$4,000,000

Dominion Virginia Power:
The Dominion Foundation Grant
$500,000

Virginia Land Conservation:
Foundation Grant
$500,000

Virginia Department of Game and Inland Fisheries (VDGIF):
National Coastal Wetlands Conservation Grant
$1,000,000

Virginia Department of Environmental Quality:
Clean Water Revolving Fund Loan
$6,000,000

CBF:
$1,000,000

TOTAL
$13,000,000

"I think that's the real story—we had this collaborative process. We helped the city understand what we were trying to do, and then we held these community meetings, so the city really became a true partner. We felt comfortable throwing just about any idea in front of them."

PAUL WILLEY
Chesapeake Bay Foundation

"It was really Will's vision," says Willey. "He believed the right thing to do was to try to preserve it, and if we could also build our center there, great."

CBF approached the Trust for Public Land, a national non-profit that specializes in acquiring land for conservation all over the United States. Lynda Frost, Project Director for TPL, walked the property with Everett, and immediately recognized its value as a rare piece of undeveloped waterfront with unobstructed public access to the water.

The project was blessed with serendipitous timing. The Recession had caught developers with holdings that depreciated overnight. L.M. Sandler & Sons foreclosed, and in 2010 ownership of the property reverted to the trustee, Wells Fargo Bank.

L.M. Sandler & Sons had paid $30 million for the property. At this point, the bank valued it at $19 million. CBF and the City of Virginia Beach came to an agreement: CBF would purchase ten acres for $1 million; the City would purchase the remaining 108 acres.

It was doubtful that the City of Virginia Beach and CBF could jointly raise $19 million, so TPL negotiated with Wells Fargo, ultimately settling on a purchase price of $13 million.

The City of Virginia Beach put $4 million from its Open Space fund on the table. Frost located and applied for several grants, including a $1 million National Coastal Wetlands Conservation grant. The terms for this grant directed the City of Virginia Beach to put most of its acreage in a conservation easement. Today, 84 of the City's 108 acres are designated as a conservation easement; the rest is a city park.

It was a win-win-win. CBF acquired a site for its new environmental center; the City added a gem to its inventory of open space; the community gained access to the site in perpetuity, and Pleasure House Point was preserved as bird and wildlife habitat.

MORE HURDLES

The preservation of the Pleasure House Point property was a great victory for CBF, the City of Virginia Beach, and the community. However, developing the site would require a conditional use permit.

This public process would give community members the chance to weigh in, and some who were enthusiastic about the preservation of Pleasure House Point were less so about the notion of a new building there, even if it was an environmental education center.

There was some misunderstanding about what CBF hoped to accomplish. Some people were concerned that CBF was going to build right on the beach or on top of wetlands. Others were concerned about increased noise and traffic, the potential loss of views, and restricted access to land they considered theirs.

Here is where CBF's strong relationship with the City of Virginia Beach paid off. Early on, Willey invited representatives from the City to travel to Annapolis to see the Merrill Center and learn more about CBF's programs.

"Before that, we were just faces in a tiny office in Norfolk," says Willey. "When they came to the Merrill Center and saw the students out in the field and people in the conference rooms, they started to see this project as a very powerful thing that was going to be part of their community."

Brian Solis of Virginia Beach Parks and Recreation helped organize public meetings, and because he and other City employees understood CBF's mission, they stood behind the organization.

CBF had another ally. When Willey and Everett needed marketing materials to present their case to the community, someone had suggested that

Willey contact Billy Almond, landscape architect and president of WPL Site Design. Almond had grown up in Virginia Beach; he knew the land and he knew the people.

CBF hired WPL to conduct a preliminary study for the possible development of an environmental center. WPL contacted Kimley-Horn, the firm that had done land development engineering for the ill-fated Indigo Dunes project. Kimley-Horn generously allowed WPL to use all the data for their study. Almond attended the stakeholder meetings, but he also met one-on-one with property owners and other community members. Christy Everett knocked on doors in hopes of winning over skeptics. She and Willey answered questions—often the same questions—at meeting after meeting. Through patience and persistence, CBF convinced the community that an environmental center would benefit not only the Bay and the children who would be attending programs there, but also the people who lived in the neighborhood next door.

29

PART II

Beyond Sustainability

Building for Resilience

Elevating the building is one of several strategies that makes the Brock Center resilient in the face of climate change. Photo: Prakash Patel

The Brock Center was designed not only to withstand the impacts of flooding, but to buffer the surrounding neighborhood from storm surges. Photo: Dave Chance

Once Pleasure House Point had been preserved, the Chesapeake Bay Foundation (CBF) could focus on designing the new Hampton Roads facility. Under Mary Tod Winchester's direction, CBF knew that it would be a leading-edge green building, one that raised the bar yet again while demonstrating exemplary renewable energy strategies, water conservation, and sustainable construction. The project also had to function as an environmental education center and teaching tool, and it had to work for CBF staff. Finally, the building needed to engage, welcome, and serve the greater community. And it had to accomplish all of these goals under challenging environmental circumstances.

The Tidewater region has been identified as the second-most vulnerable region in the United States, after New Orleans, to the predicted impacts of climate change. These impacts, which include rising sea levels and more frequent and severe storms, are already occurring in Hampton Roads. Average sea level has risen over fourteen inches since 1930 and extreme rainfall events have increased by 33 percent over the last 60 years.

Flooding is a fact of life in Hampton Roads, and the problem is exacerbated by conventional development, which adds more impervious surfaces in the form of buildings, roads, and parking lots. One hundred percent of the Pleasure House Point site lies in a high-risk flood zone. Any building constructed there would have to be able to withstand the battering winds, driving rain, and powerful storm surges of the locale; it also needed to remain above rising sea levels. In practical terms, this meant elevating the building and constructing it with durable, strong materials. CBF wanted to set an example with a building that works with and responds to nature, especially with regard to stormwater, which is an important policy issue for the organization. CBF also wanted to demonstrate good construction practices that exceeded the minimums required by code.

Greg Mella of SmithGroupJJR had stayed in contact with Winchester over the years. When he learned about CBF's plan to build a new environmental education center, he planted a veritable seed.

"Mary Tod stated the new building must be at least LEED Platinum; it had to go beyond the Merrill Center," says Mella. "I said, 'well, there's this thing called the Living Building Challenge.' In a lot of ways, the LBC is today what LEED Platinum was in 2001."

Winchester had also heard about the Living Building Challenge from green building pioneer Rob Watson, and she promoted the program to the Task Force and Leadership Council. Paul Willey and Janet Harrison began learning about the Living Building Challenge. They attended an introductory workshop in New York City in fall of 2011, and Harrison began putting together a reference guide from the ILFI Dialogue. In April 2012, Harrison officially registered the project under Living Building Challenge 2.1.

Photo: Courtesy Skanska USA

> *"People recognized that this project represented the best of what we do: hands-on education that fosters greater awareness of the Bay; on-site restoration; and community engagement and collaboration. If we hadn't conceived of a facility that did all three of these things, it wouldn't have been so compelling to so many people."*
>
> **KATE WILSON**
> Chesapeake Bay Foundation

SUPPORTING THE VISION

During the search for land, CBF organized the Hampton Roads Leadership Council. This group brought together twenty-five community leaders, some of whom served on CBF's Board of Directors, to further the vision for the environmental center.

Included in the Council was Harry Lester, who had long advocated for CBF to increase its presence in Virginia. The Council's primary charge was to assist CBF as advisors, advocates, and volunteer fundraisers for the project.

"The Leadership Council was critical to the project's success," says Kate Wilson, Director of Principal and Major Giving for CBF in Virginia. "Everyone on the Council supported the project

financially, but members also helped navigate strategic conversations with key members of the Hampton Roads community."

Christy Everett organized regular meetings with the Leadership Council. These meetings included updates on policy, education, outreach and advocacy in the Hampton Roads region. Recognizing the potential of the project to support the important work of CBF in Hampton

Roads, several donors made significant contributions before the Pleasure House Point property was acquired and before the programmatic and building campaign was officially launched.

Jane Batten, a local philanthropist and member of the Leadership Council, made one such early donation. Her gift was directed into an endowment fund. The fund and its annual returns were slated to support the operation of the Hampton Roads facility and its educational programs in perpetuity.

Leadership Council member Macon Brock and his wife Joan Brock also made a major early contribution. Lifetime Hampton Roads residents, the Brocks had witnessed the decline of The Chesapeake Bay and its rivers over the decades, and they were long-time supporters of environmental and educational initiatives. The new building was christened the Brock Environmental Center in recognition of the couple's generosity and commitment to conservation.

In October 2012, CBF announced a $21 million comprehensive campaign that would fund the acquisition, development and restoration of the site, the construction of the environmental center, and support CBF's Hampton Roads programs and staff.

In 2013, CBF invited the public to participate in the creation of the Brock Environmental Center with its "Raise the Roof" campaign.

"We wanted a way for people in the community, who were so emotionally invested in the place and the project, to participate, regardless of capacity," says Wilson. Donors could purchase a zinc roof tile, either in their names or in honor of a loved one. Today, the tiles are displayed along the entire length of one wall of the Brock Environmental Center's conference room.

Fundraising continued through design, construction, and the first year of occupation.

Joan & Macon Brock
Photo: Glen McClure, courtesy The Hampton Roads Community Foundation

"The Brock Center has already been highly successful. It has exceeded our expectations and is doing what it was intended to do—expressing CBF's mission in the South Bay and educating young people on environmental issues. We take the philosophy that you're wasting your time with older people; they are already set in their ways. But if you can educate the younger generation, they will grow up to be better older people."

MACON BROCK
CBF Board Member

35

CHESAPEAKE BAY FOUNDATION HAMPTON ROADS LEADERSHIP COUNCIL

"The Task Force and Leadership Council were amazingly supportive. We had come up with a budget before we decided to pursue the Living Building Challenge. Nobody had any idea how much that was going to cost. But they were adamant that we weren't going to cut any of the green agenda."

PAUL WILLEY
Chesapeake Bay Foundation

"If I did anything, it was to convince the CBF Board that Virginia was the forgotten stepchild. I like to say, Maryland may have the Bay, but down in Virginia we have the Bay and the ocean. Now CBF has two environmental centers—one in Maryland and one in Virginia Beach—that are like bookends. With the help of CBF and the State's school superintendent, all of these kids in Virginia now have the opportunity to come and touch the water. And when you get rid of all the noise, that's what it's all about."

HARRY LESTER
CBF Board of Trustees Chair

Once CBF had focused on the Pleasure House Point property, Winchester and Paul Willey created a smaller Task Force that drew in part from the Leadership Council. Members were selected because of their connections with the design and construction industry; they included Rob Kinsley, Preston White, Bob Wells, Lucius Kellam, and George Clarke. The Task Force was charged with selecting the architecture and engineering firm and the construction manager for the building project, and for providing general project oversight throughout design and construction. The group also advised CBF on pricing, and helped decide which features to possibly cut or scale back during the value engineering process. The project's green features, however, were non-negotiable.

Architect Janet Harrison served as an advisor to the Task Force and, later, Jane Batten was brought in to consult on the final design. CBF President Will Baker also participated on major decisions.

"When the Brock Center opportunity came up, there was no way we weren't going to get as much of the team back together as we could. We brought with us recognition of the lessons learned from Merrill Center. We knew the clients, and we knew how to leverage their internal talents."

CINDY COGIL
SmithGroupJJR

A FRUITFUL PARTNERSHIP

In April 2011, CBF announced a Request for Qualifications (RFQ) for architectural and engineering services for the Hampton Roads project. More than two dozen firms responded. CBF solicited proposals from three of these firms, one of which was SmithGroupJJR.

Founded in 1853, SmithGroupJJR is the longest continually practicing architecture and engineering firm in the United States. Since designing CBF's Merrill Center, SmithGroupJJR had added sixty-seven LEED-certified projects to its portfolio, and over half of the firm's 800 staff members were LEED accredited.

Other "firsts" included the first LEED Platinum federal building—the Science & Technology Facility built for the National Renewable Energy Laboratory (NREL) in Golden, Colorado—and the first LEED Platinum dormitory in the world, located at Duke University in Durham, North Carolina.

In the years since becoming the Merrill Center's spokespersons, Greg Mella and engineer Cindy Cogil had enjoyed parallel careers. Each became principals within three years, and they collaborated on several projects, including the Sandhill Research Center at Clemson University and Goodpaster Hall at St. Mary's College in Maryland.

Mella had developed into an architect specializing in designing sustainable and LEED-certified projects for sensitive habitats, including The Chesapeake Bay. He was also learning about the Living Building Challenge. He had invited Jason F. McLennan to participate in his firm's annual Sustainability Retreat; shortly afterward, Mella went through the training to become a Living Building Challenge Ambassador.

SmithGroupJJR offers comprehensive services, including landscape architecture and civil engineering. For this project, SmithGroupJJR brought WPL Site Design on board as the landscape architect and civil engineer of record.

SmithGroupJJR presented to CBF at the Merrill Center, in a room overlooking The Chesapeake Bay. The presentation was built around the Living Building Challenge and highlighted the firm's competitive advantages: its long-standing relationship with CBF, a significant portfolio of leading-edge sustainable projects, including the Merrill Center, and the effective partnership between Mella and Cogil.

"We went in with design ideas but no built form," says Mella. "Instead, we talked more about approaches and strategies."

A month after their presentation, CBF informed SmithGroupJJR that they had been selected.

"A lot of people thought we hired SmithGroupJJR because they did the Merrill Center, but that's not what happened," says Winchester. "They were up against some very competitive architecture firms."

37

(Front row) Amanda Sturgeon, Chris Gorri, Janet Harrison, Mary Tod Winchester, Pete Muñoz and Dafeng Cai (Back Row) Willy Agee, Greg Mella, Megan O'Connell, Erica Nachman, Tyler Park, Russell Perry, Jason F. McLennan. Photo: Courtesy ILFI

THE TEAM GELS

Despite CBF's experience building facilities, Winchester knew they were in new territory.

As the sustainability consultant and a vital advisor to the CBF Task Force, architect Janet Harrison was leading the effort to learn as much about the Living Building Challenge as possible before embarking on the design process.

Before selecting the Construction Manager, CBF had also hired Skanska, an international construction management firm, to act as owner's representative. At the time, few firms had any experience with the Living Building Challenge. Skanska had served as the builder for the Bertschi School Living Building Science Wing, the first project to achieve full certification under Living Building

Challenge v2.0, and was collaborating with SERA on a second Living Building Challenge project in Portland, Oregon.

As the owner's representative, Skanska provided overall project management, with duties ranging from contract negotiation and the selection of the Construction Manager to design review and budget reconciliation. Later, Skanska provided on-site quality control and consulted on the Red List requirements tied to materials selection.

Curtis Elswick, Vice President of Skanska Integrated Solutions, helped facilitate planning and design on the front end of the project. Elizabeth Heider, then Senior Vice President for Green Markets for Skanska USA, brought deep green experience to the team, as an advocate for leading-edge building technologies with long involvement with the U.S. Green Building Council. Heider participated in the design charrettes, helping ensure that CBF

> *"It was a terrific opportunity to work with an amazing client, to build something that would be like a pebble in a pond—that had the potential to create incredible ripples that would expand way beyond the building."*

ELIZABETH HEIDER
Skanska USA

> *"When we started imagining the project, Greg and I both recognized the potential of these projects to be benchmarks, models and gamechangers, each one building on the last. So we came up with the idea of the Design Advisory Group (or Board). We thought that, with this group and the already mature relationship Greg and Cindy enjoyed with CBF, we could create the intellectual setting for something quite special."*

RUS PERRY
SmithGroupJJR

met its sustainability goals. Later, Project Engineer Megan O'Connell provided hand-on materials vetting, and Doug Erck came on during construction to serve as Skanska's eyes and ears on the site.

SmithGroupJJR hired WPL Site Design as the civil engineer and landscape architect. WPL had been involved through the land acquisition and had developed both the Feasibility Study for CBF and the Master Plan for the City of Virginia Beach. The firm's experience with cutting-edge water systems would also help meet the requirements of the Water Petal. Billy Almond, with his deep local roots, was a vital link to the Virginia Beach community.

GOALS AND VISION

Mella asked Rus Perry to serve as principal for this exciting and ground-breaking project. Together, the two served as Co-Directors of Sustainable Design for SmithGroupJJR. However, Perry was adamant that Mella and Cindy Cogil should serve as principal architect and engineer for the Brock Center.

Perry was still to have a meaningful role in the project. He and Mella put together a "dream team" of leading sustainability thinkers called the Design Advisory Group, which originally included Perry, Jason F. McLennan, and Rob Watson. Once Skanska was hired as owner's representative, Elizabeth Heider was invited to join the group, as well.

Perry was leading the charge advocating for greater materials transparency. Before joining SmithGroupJJR in 2005, he was in partnership with Bill McDonough, who developed the Cradle to Cradle protocol with Michael Braungart, and he was a founding member of the Health Product Declaration Collaborative.

Heider, who grew up in Tidewater, had long been an advocate for leading-edge green building strategies. In 2013, after twelve years with Skanska USA, she was hired for the newly created position of Chief Sustainability Officer. McLennan, creator of the Living Building Challenge, was serving as CEO of the International Living Future Institute (ILFI) at the time. Watson, former president of the U.S. Green Building Council who is often credited as the "Father of LEED," had also founded the ECON Group, which focuses on optimizing buildings' lifetime performance.

The Design Advisory Group advised the team on strategy and goals during two design charrettes—one at the beginning of the design process and a second during Schematic Design—but did not participate directly in the actual design.

Each member brought special strengths to the table: Perry with his background in materials transparency and green chemistry; Heider with her experience in cost estimating and building longevity; Watson with his expertise in systems and energy performance; and McLennan with his uncanny ability to see big-picture opportunities and push a project beyond sustainability and into the realm of regenerative design.

"The yin and yang was pretty interesting," says Perry. "Jason will drift off into some very spiritual places, but Rob wanted to know where the air is moving; he's all about kBTUs."

> *"We knew the Living Building Challenge was a new world. We wanted to show how interested we were in being part of that new world."*

CHRIS BRANDT
Hourigan Construction

> *"One of the keys to the success of this project was that CBF was able to bring their design-build team on board from the beginning. It was very forward-thinking of CBF, and something we don't see here at the City."*

BRIAN SOLIS
City of Virginia Beach

DOING THE HOMEWORK

Once SmithGroupJJR had been selected, CBF moved immediately to the task of selecting a Construction Manager. From her experience with the Merrill Center, Winchester had learned how important it was to have the team together at the beginning of design.

CBF sent RFQs to a dozen construction firms before narrowing the field to three. They hoped to find one rooted in the region, with a portfolio of projects focused on sustainability and a willingness to embrace the Living Building Challenge. Under the Task Force's guidance, CBF weighed many factors, including the firm's location, environmental track record, RFQ submittals, and references.

CBF awarded Virginia-based Hourigan Construction the contract for Construction Manager for the Brock Environmental Center, citing the company's combination of experience, passion, and insight into what would be required to meet the high standards of the Living Building Challenge.

Led by President Mark Hourigan, Hourigan Construction is an award-winning construction firm that specializes in commercial and institutional buildings. The firm has been an early adopter of Building Information Modeling (BIM), the 3-D virtual construction software that facilitates collaboration among designers, engineers, contractors and sub-contractors.

Although Hourigan had a solid portfolio of LEED-certified projects, the firm was unfamiliar with the Living Building Challenge. Executive Vice President Chris Brandt, who was to serve as Project Executive, made it his team's job to learn as much as they could about the program before their presentation. Consequently, Hourigan proposed something that no other firm did: that they would assign a full-time Quality Control Manager to be in charge of materials. "We studied the program enough to know it couldn't be managed like a regular project," says Brandt. "We tried to make that clear in our presentation."

An experienced project manager, Brandt also led the firm's efforts to mentor students from Virginia Tech's Department of Building Construction throughout the project. Larry Ramsay served as Project Manager, while Thomas Jackson acted as Project Superintendent. Virtual Construction Coordinator Michael Henley led the BIM effort, and a young hire named Tyler Park served as QCM and Assistant Project Manager.

40

The design charrette kicked off with a site visit to Pleasure House Point.
Photo: Courtesy Hourigan Construction

AN EPIC DESIGN CHARRETTE

On April 11, 2012, the team met at the Pleasure House Point site to kick off an all-day design charrette. Participating were representatives from SmithGroupJJR, Hourigan Construction, Skanska and WPL Site Design. Paul Willey, Christy Everett, and Mary Tod Winchester from CBF and Brian Solis and Barry Frankenfield from the City of Virginia Beach were also present, as were Jason F. McLennan, Elizabeth Heider, and Rus Perry from the Design Advisory Group.

For some, it was their first introduction to the landscape. Walking the paths through forest, meadow, and marsh, hearing the birds, feeling the maritime breezes, and taking in the expansive views of The Chesapeake Bay helped people connect to the place in a very real way, and it set the tone for the rest of the day.

The rest of the charrette was held at a conference room at a nearby state park. There the team discussed strategies for fulfilling each of the Living Building Challenge Petal requirements and siting of the project elements, which included the building, education pavilion, parking, and other infrastructure.

"We had no concepts on paper before the charrette," says Mella. "We felt it was important to figure out what we wanted the building to do before we knew what it would look like."

SmithGroupJJR and WPL had compiled a site analysis, including aerial photos, which helped the team identify developable areas and targets

"Visiting the site at this early stage, and being a part of the charrette, I felt so motivated and engaged for the rest of the project. It's easy to lose focus of the big picture—of the original vision and goals. Seeing the site and being inspired by it, and connecting with everyone on the team helped me keep my eye on the prize the whole way through."

SARA LAPPANO
SmithGroupJJR

41

"The entire group was so focused on the bigger goal. It lifted our spirits and we kept our eye on that elevated prize. It was a mash-up of all of these things dear to my heart. It wasn't just about the act of designing or building another building; it was a spiritual experience."

ELIZABETH HEIDER
Skanska USA

"We know each other's stories so well by now. I can do a whole architectural presentation and talk about natural daylighting schemes; the lead architect can talk about construction practices and how the nuts and bolts fit together."

TYLER PARK
Hourigan Construction

'We wouldn't have gotten there if all the people involved hadn't been of like mind. We have the right goal in mind, and we're all decent enough people to work together. And that's what it's all about: the people. In every case it's about the people. And in this case, I think the right people chose the right people —so we could all work together."

CHRIS BRANDT
Hourigan Construction

"There are great construction teams, and when they get together, they shake hands and sit down. When we get together, 90 percent of it is hugs, because it was that deep."

TYLER PARK
Hourigan Construction

for active restoration. They had also prepared a climate analysis and details about proposed building systems.

Sensitive to the feedback they had received from the community, CBF expressed two very significant concerns: How visitors were going to access the site, and how development was going to impact the site.

"We were very concerned about building on Pleasure House Point," says Winchester. "One of the first questions we asked Jason [McLennan] was, 'Is it okay to build here?'"

McLennan showed the team a sketch he had drawn while walking the site. It depicted a one-story building hugging the maritime forest and buffering the rest of the site from the neighborhood. Most of the land was left to perform its ecological role.

"Buildings are often vilified by their very existence as being a bad thing, from an environmental perspective," says Heider. "With his sketch, Jason changed the calculus of the discussion, introducing the concept that the building could actually do more good than bad."

McLennan encouraged the team to consider the next larger scale, and to imagine the entire site as stormwater treatment for the surrounding neighborhood. With this in mind, McLennan addressed the problem of the parking lot. His solution: there should not be one on the site at all. This radical suggestion gave CBF permission to ponder possibilities it had never considered. One of these was the option of using Marlin Bay Drive, a road that had been widened to serve the Indigo Dunes development, as on-street parking to serve the environmental center.

Jason F. McLennan illustrates his ideas during the Brock Center design charrette.

The Brock Team during a site visit to the Bullitt
Center, then under construction, in Seattle, Wash.
Photo: Courtesy Hourigan Construction

"There was so much value in having this outside perspective," says Everett. "I was amazed that during the charrette the problem of parking just got solved." Of course, CBF still had to sell the idea to the City of Virginia Beach, but now they had the philosophical justification to do so.

Following the charrette, it made sense for the team to attend the Living Future unConference in Portland, Oregon. Along with a dose of inspiration, the conference would provide an opportunity to talk with other project teams.

The team first flew to Seattle, where team members toured two Living Building Challenge projects: the completed Bertschi School and the Bullitt Center, then under construction. The team also attended a debriefing session at Miller-Hull's office before heading to Portland for the conference. There the team met with architects from SERA and representatives from Skanska USA. The two firms were collaborating on the Oregon Sustainability Center, a Living Building Project that unfortunately was never built.

"We bonded, and we also learned what we were in for," says Mella. "That's when we realized the Red List was going to be a challenge."

After an exhilarating and exhausting odyssey, the team members returned to the East Coast. It was time to roll up their sleeves and get to work.

43

"We kept looking at curves, whether it was the oyster shell or terrapin or the curving limbs of the live oak. We wanted the building's form to reflect nature. We wanted it to reflect the spirit of the place, to reflect the various indigenous cultures that shaped it. We wanted it to draw on cues from the site, from nature, and from the work that CBF does."

GREG MELLA
SmithGroupJJR

THE BUILDING TAKES SHAPE

Before the charrette, SmithGroupJJR had met with a large group from CBF for a visioning session. Based on feedback from the session, the team members came up with a list of concepts and descriptors they hoped the Brock Environmental Center would embody.

One of the most important of these was the concept of invisibility. The building should visually blend into the site, but its impact should also be invisible, or neutral. It should connect to both the region's ecology and its cultural history, which prompted an exploration of indigenous buildings, such as the longhouse and the kiva. Biophilia and biomimicry also emerged as design drivers. As the team began exploring shapes inspired by nature, they were drawn to curving forms native to Pleasure House Point: the limbs of live oaks; and the shells of oysters and diamondback terrapins. In fact, they began thinking of the entire building as a native creature: a heron or other waterbird on long legs, with a definite "head" and "tail."

Coming out of the charrette and the ILFI unConference, the team had also identified several key elements that would contribute to the building's sustainability, and that would significantly influence the design.

- Rainwater collection would affect roof shape and material selection

- Passive solar design and building orientation would influence the amount and placement of glazing as well as shading strategies

- Natural ventilation would affect the shape and orientation of the building and the location of windows

- Daylighting would affect the shape of the building, amount and location of windows and shading

- Renewable energy strategies (solar PV and wind) would affect the siting and orientation of the building and the shape of the roof

- Composting toilets would require elevating the building

At one point CBF had asked for a separate education pavilion, but to lessen the project's footprint, CBF and SmithGroupJJR decided to consolidate all elements into one building, and to use the lobby to separate offices from the more public events facilities.

Integrating all of these ideas, the building began to take shape: a long, narrow, curving form that reflected the horizontality of the site. The shape expanded into a multi-purpose room at the west end, where visitors would first encounter the building. This multi-purpose room itself was envisioned as another curved form—a celebration of biomimicry and biophilia—even though its exact shape was still to be determined.

Although the building went through several iterations, its basic form was preserved in the final design.

44

BUILDING FLOORPLAN

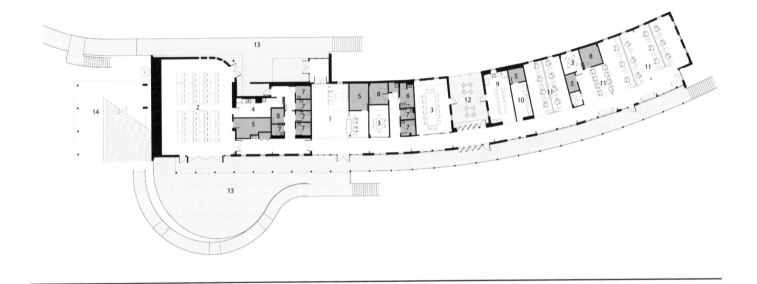

1. LOBBY
2. CONFERENCE ROOM
3. MEETING ROOM
4. CATERING KITCHEN
5. STORAGE
6. STAFF SHOWER
7. W/C
8. MECHANICAL ROOM
9. STAFF DINING ROOM
10. COPY ROOM
11. OFFICES
12. DOG TROT
13. DECK/PORCH
14. EDUCATION PAVILION (BELOW)

A deeply integrated design process was key to meeting the Brock Center's ambitious goals. Photo: Dave Chance

"What is unique to our team—and this was true for both the Merrill Center and Brock—is that the architect and the engineer sit steps away from each other, which facilitates collaboration. Being under one roof allowed us to work as one team, and it made the design process very fluid."

GREG MELLA
SmithGroupJJR

"I will never be more proud of a project than I am of the CBF Brock Environmental Center. All of us—the architects, the engineers, the CBF and the City of Virginia Beach—were 'all in' from Day One. It was truly a collaborative effort from everyone involved."

LARRY RAMSAY
Hourigan Construction

COLLABORATION ON ALL FRONTS

A project with such ambitious sustainability goals as the Brock Environmental Center required intensive collaboration and frequent communication—a truly integrated approach.

The project would not have happened without the partnership between CBF and the City of Virginia Beach, and the two entities continued to work together as CBF navigated the obstacles to accomplishing their sustainability goals. The solid relationship made it much easier for Willey and Everett to approach city officials with requests, and the City more receptive to new and advanced design approaches without local precedent.

Within CBF, the Hampton Roads Leadership Council and Task Force provided financial support, vital connections with the larger community, and practical guidance through design and construction.

Weekly calls with CBF, the architect and contractor began early on and continued for three years. This close collaboration between SmithGroupJJR and Hourigan, especially Hourigan's advising on pricing, ensured that the budget stayed on track and helped the team meet the stringent requirements of the Materials Petal.

Janet Harrison worked closely with Paul Willey of CBF to develop RFPs, process submittals, and schedule interviews. As point person for the Living Building Challenge and LEED requirements, Harrison made herself available to answer questions; if she did not know the answer, she would seek one. Once the team dug into

the Red List requirements in earnest, Harrison worked closely with architect Dafeng Cai of SmithGroupJJR and Tyler Park of Hourigan Construction, with support from Elizabeth Heider of Skanska. Later, Sydney Covey, Sustainability Analyst with Hourigan Construction, was also brought on to help with materials vetting and Living Building Challenge certification.

During design/development, Cindy Cogil was offered a new position in SmithGroupJJR's Chicago office. She left the project in the capable hands of Electrical Engineer Sara Lappano and Mechanical Engineer Brian Coffield. Mella brought Cai on board to prepare construction documents, conduct 3-D modeling, and take on materials vetting.

SmithGroupJJR enjoys the distinct advantage of having both architects and engineers under one roof. The firm's integrated approach is reflected in their office's seating configuration, where staff are grouped in teams, rather than by discipline. Having Lappano and Coffield involved early in the design process was critical for success in meeting the net zero energy, water, and waste goals. The team implemented a performance-based design process, using simulation tools to test design ideas. This integrated process required all team members to be nimble and work together, but it also enabled them to draw on synergies between strategies—and ultimately, to optimize the building's performance.

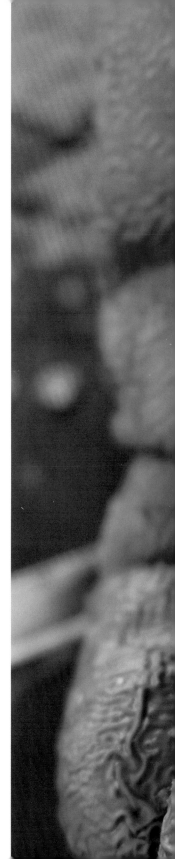

PART III

Rising to the Challenge

Addressing Each Petal of
the Living Building Challenge

48

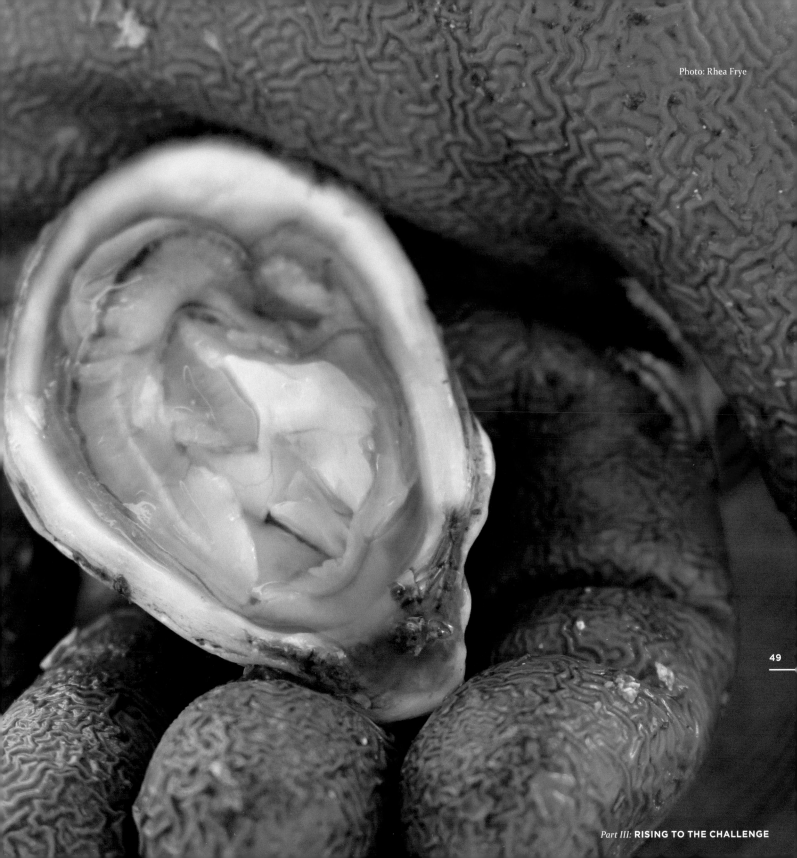

49

Part III: **RISING TO THE CHALLENGE**

"*Imagine a building constructed to function as elegantly and efficiently as a flower; a building informed by its bioregion's characteristics, and that generates all of its own energy with renewable resources, captures and treats all of its water, and operates efficiently and for maximum beauty.*"

LIVING BUILDING CHALLENGE VERSION 2.1

The following seven chapters focus on the individual Petals of the Living Building Challenge:

1. SITE   5. MATERIALS

2. WATER   6. EQUITY

3. ENERGY   7. BEAUTY

4. HEALTH

Although the chapters in this section are presented in the order that they appear in Living Building Challenge 2.1, the process of design and construction was not so linear; instead, project teams often contemplated many Imperatives at once, and stories that appear in one chapter could easily fall under another chapter. For more information on the seven Petals and twenty Imperatives of the Living Building Challenge, please visit **living-future.org**.

THE
SITE
PETAL

Deep Sense of Place

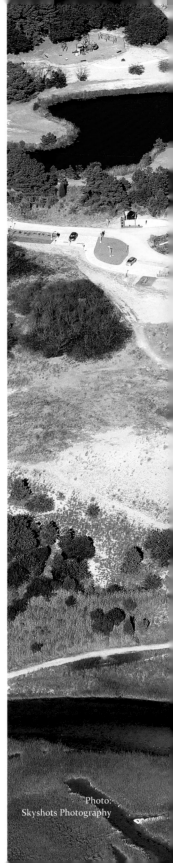

Photo:
Skyshots Photography

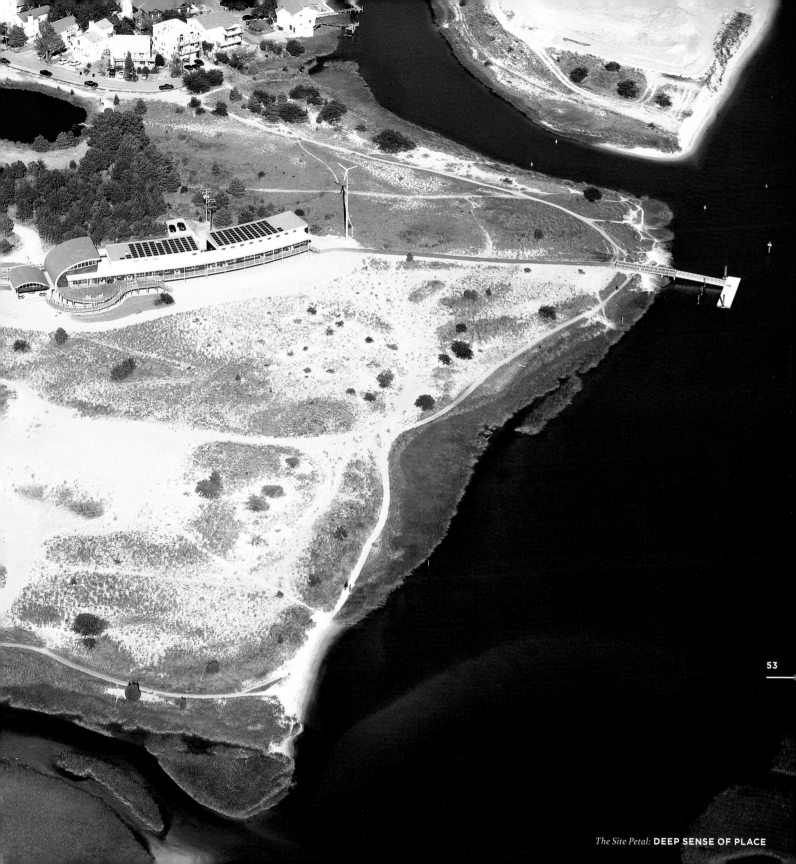

The Site Petal: **DEEP SENSE OF PLACE**

SUMMARY OF THE LIVING BUILDING CHALLENGE VERSION 2.1 SITE PETAL

Petal Intent

The intent of the Site Petal is to clearly articulate where it is acceptable for people to build, how to protect and restore a place once it has been developed, and to encourage the creation of communities that are once again based on the pedestrian rather than the automobile. Such communities should, in turn, be supported by local and regional agriculture, since no truly "sustainable" community can exist that relies on globally-sourced food production.

Petal Imperatives

- Limits To Growth
- Urban Agriculture
- Habitat Exchange
- Car Free Living

The Brock Center is located on CBF's ten acres; most of Pleasure House Point has been preserved as a public park. Photo: Dave Chance

The intent of the Site Petal, simply stated, is to "restore a healthy coexistence with nature." A prevailing attitude about the built environment is that its impacts on the natural world, even when minimized, will always be negative. The Brock Environmental Center invites visitors to view human development in a different light—as something that can work with natural processes to actively restore ecosystems and enhance the connections between people and the natural world.

The Brock site falls under Transect L1: Natural Habitat Preserve. This most restrictive category includes land that is set aside as a nature preserve or defined as "sensitive ecological habitat." The Living Building Challenge Standard only allows development that is related to the preservation or interpretation of the landscape in this transect. Both of these actions fall under CBF's mission. Still, once the Pleasure House Point property had been saved from being developed with condominiums, CBF struggled with the question of whether or not it was appropriate to build there.

55

"The whole project also addresses the underlying issues of climate change and sea level rise by showing how we can build with a zero carbon footprint. Not only does it provide a good example of how to build, but the whole purpose of the project is to spread the word and teach school children and the public about these environmental issues in the hopes of making a difference."

JANET HARRISON
J. Harrison Architects

At first glance, there were several valid arguments against building on Pleasure House Point. The site is in the floodplain. Much of it consists of filled wetlands. Limits to Growth, the very first Imperative in the Living Building Challenge 2.1 Standard, clearly states that no project may be constructed within the 100-year floodplain. Why would an environmental advocacy organization choose such a site?

Jason F. McLennan insisted that Pleasure House Point was the best place for a new environmental center, precisely because of the access it provided to the natural habitat. Having the support of ILFI boosted CBF's resolve and helped the organization build a compelling case. Locating the Center on an ecologically sensitive site allows CBF to implement its advocacy, restoration, and education efforts all in one location. An environmental center on Pleasure House Point would bring people to The Chesapeake Bay. As CBF educators well know, when people have access to a resource—when they can see it, smell it, and touch it—they are more willing and motivated to preserve it. In addition, the Brock Environmental Center was designed to be a regenerative building. The project would not only minimize negative impacts, it would restore and protect ecological processes, create and protect wildlife habitat, and treat stormwater, to the benefit of the entire neighborhood. It would serve as an inspiring example of what is possible.

Building on the site required a Conditional Use Permit from the City of Virginia Beach, so for this reason it was also important to have community support for the project. Mary Tod Winchester and her colleagues were well aware that some members of the Virginia Beach community were taken aback by the idea, however false, that CBF wanted to build an environmental center "on top of wetlands."

Fortunately, CBF and the City had built up significant goodwill as they worked together to jointly acquire Pleasure House Point. CBF and the City hosted several public meetings in order to answer questions about the proposed building, and Paul Willey, Christy Everett, and Billy Almond met with many community members one-on-one in order to allay fears and clear up misconceptions.

The Habitat Exchange Imperative requires that, for each hectare of development, project teams must set aside an equal area of land in perpetuity. CBF chose a project through the Living Future Habitat Exchange Program in order to fulfill this requirement, but the preservation of Pleasure House Point is itself a story about habitat exchange: saving 110 acres of habitat from development, restoring its ecological functions, and introducing thousands of people to its ecology and beauty.

A RESILIENT LANDSCAPE

Pleasure House Point was originally a partially forested inlet with tidal marshlands, which later was included in the Newton Estate. While certainly not pristine, the site had never been developed with buildings.

In the 1950s, the Army Corps of Engineers began using the site as a repository for dredge spoils, effectively turning it into a greyfield. The agency built a dike to separate dewatering ponds from the tidal creeks.

Over the years, people in the neighboring community had claimed the site as their own, and it was a favored spot for recreationists who liked to fish off the point, walk along the shoreline, and wind through the dunes on ATVS. Over the years, all of this activity carved a network of informal trails through the site.

Once the dumping ceased in the 1990s, the land began to heal itself. As the dikes eroded, breaches in the ponds restored a connection between these burgeoning marshes and tidal flows. Native grasses began colonizing the area.

The area just inland of Pleasure House Point had been most impacted by the dumping of dredge spoils, but salt meadows began to thrive, and small shrubs and trees crept in from the maritime forest. This forest, which comprises the northern portion of the acreage, includes Loblolly Pine, Red Oak, Live Oak, Black Cherry, and Black Gum.

As with many estuarine environments, Pleasure House Point is rich wildlife habitat. At least 122 species of birds have been identified nesting, foraging, or passing through during migration. The northern diamond-backed terrapin, so called for the diamond-shaped growth rings that decorate its top shell, uses the property for nesting and foraging, primarily within one hundred feet of the edge of the tidal waters. This federally designated Species of Special Concern is the only turtle that lives exclusively in brackish water. A 2010 survey identified 113 terrapin nests along the eastern shoreline of Pleasure House Point.

The Diamondback Terrapin nests on the sandy beaches of Pleasure House Point.
Photo: Judy Ullmann

Pervious pavers, used to construct parking areas and walkways, help prevent stormwater runoff. Photo: Billy Almond.

SITING RIGHT

The Brock Center was sited to minimize impacts to the recovering landscape. This site decision included limiting development beyond two hundred feet of the wetlands and shoreline—a buffer twice the size of what was required. CBF wanted to set an example that shows the benefits of going beyond what is simply required by code.

This buffer protects water quality, allows revegetation of the shoreline to continue, and respects the fluid dynamics of the shoreline environment.

Building in the floodplain meant having to anticipate future events, including 100-year storms that would flood the entire site. In addition, the EPA estimates that by the year 2100, sea level in Hampton Roads will have risen nearly three feet. To protect the Brock Environmental Center from flooding and future sea level rise, the building is elevated nearly fourteen feet above sea level. It is built on the area that had seen the most build-up of dredge spoils, which precluded having to import more material. The site elements, including the main building, fire lane, wind turbines, and limited parking, are clustered together on the northeastern

portion of the site, along the edge of the successional maritime forest. The trees provide an important visual buffer between the Brock Center and homes located to the north.

CBF set a goal of no more than 10 percent effective impervious area for the entire project. Accomplishing this target required finding alternatives to conventional paving materials and the extensive use of stormwater management best practices. Even the road connecting the Brock Center to Chesterfield Avenue is constructed of permeable pavers.

In addition, Hourigan Construction went to great lengths to minimize impacts to the site during construction. Workers parked off-site most of the time, bringing vehicles onto the site only for deliveries.

A MASTER PLAN

Beyond simply saving Pleasure House Point from conventional development, CBF and the City of Virginia Beach wanted to restore the marshland, which included reestablishing the connections between the marshes and tidal flows from Pleasure House Creek and Crab Creek.

WPL Site Design was contracted to develop a Master Plan for the entire site, which includes CBF's ten acres and the new passive park managed by the City of Virginia Beach. The plan addresses wildlife habitat and water quality, and balances the goal of providing public access with the need to minimize impacts to plants and wildlife.

Time is one of the key ingredients in this plan. CBF plans to maintain as much of the site in a natural state as possible, encouraging the ecological processes that are already in place. These successive processes include the colonization of tidal and non-tidal marshes by native grasses, and the establishment of opportunistic Live Oaks and Southern Red Oaks in the interior.

Simply removing vehicles from the site has fast-tracked the regeneration of wetlands and dunes. Defining, formalizing, and in some cases moving trails has also reduced the physical compaction and trampling of vegetation that was trying to establish itself. Locations for both the work boat pier and

kayak launch pier were chosen to minimize the amount of marsh traversed.

CBF's more active measures includes the removal and management of invasive species such as Japanese Sedge, Mimosa, and Phragmides, an aggressive reed. Staff are also harvesting seeds from the salt meadows, in hopes of augmenting its expansion, and have planted native species in the bioswale and rain gardens.

Although the Urban Agriculture Imperative does not apply to L1 transect sites, CBF is planting species such as native blackberry that will provide food (and habitat) for wildlife. CBF is also establishing and augmenting oyster reefs in the waters surrounding Pleasure House Point. Along with the valuable ecosystem service of filtering sediment, the oyster reefs also provide opportunities for schoolchildren to learn and for volunteers to actively participate in the restoration of The Chesapeake Bay.

The two hundred-foot buffer between the building and the water is twice that which is required. Photo: Hourigan Construction

The Site Petal: **DEEP SENSE OF PLACE**

60

Photo: Chris Gorri

BROCK ENVIRONMENTAL CENTER FOR A LIVING CHESAPEAKE

IMPERATIVE:
CAR FREE LIVING

The Car Free Living Imperative states that the project should contribute towards the creation of walkable, pedestrian-oriented communities. Neither CBF nor SmithGroupJJR wanted visitors' first experience to be that of a parking lot, yet the Brock Center was designed with a conference room that seats up to eighty people, and the reality is that the Hampton Roads is a car-centric region with less than optimal public transportation. Where was everyone going to park?

Jason F. McLennan's inspired vision for how the site would function—a vision which did not include a parking lot—solved one problem but created another. Christy Everett and Paul Willey were tasked with solving it. During one of their meetings with the City of Virginia Beach, they inquired about a city-owned vacant lot next to a pump station. Could CBF use it for staff and visitor parking? Another creative solution for the parking problem had already been constructed. Marlin Bay Drive, a four-lane divided "road to nowhere," had been sized in anticipation of the Indigo Dunes condominium project. What if people parked along the little-used outbound lanes?

Parking in either location would require passing through City-owned land to access the CBF site. During that same meeting, Christy and Paul asked if CBF could build a path through the city park. To their great surprise, the City was receptive to all of these ideas.

Other than three ADA spaces, there is no parking at the Brock Environmental Center. CBF partnered with the City of Virginia Beach to create community parking north of the site, which serves both the passive park and CBF's parcel, and which includes preferred spaces for fuel-efficient vehicles and carpoolers. In a beautiful example of creative reuse, simple re-striping transformed the outbound lanes of Marlin Bay Drive into eighty viable parking spaces. From there, visitors walk along a 700-foot wooded path to access the Brock Center and its facilities. (An electric shuttle is available for larger events.) The transition is seamless; there are no fences. As the woods enclose you and the sounds of vehicles and the neighborhoods fade, the senses are filled with the sounds and smells of the forest, the marsh, and The Chesapeake Bay itself.

"We knew we were building something we wanted hundreds of people to experience. If you look at our audience, they range from the young to the old. There's a certain level of comfort we need to provide. This car free living was something we had to get comfortable with first, then we had to take it to the CBF leadership and help them get comfortable with it. I remember the parking decision was a big crossroads. This LBC direction hinged on car free living, yet we're so car-connected. I remember drawing out distance maps of the Merrill Center and comparing it to the distances walked at this site, just to help people realize that it's not that far."

PAUL WILLEY
Chesapeake Bay Foundation

"Looking back at the feasibility study developed before our team was engaged in the project, the graphic implies the design centered on parking and accommodating parking on the site—almost as if the building was a backdrop for a parking lot. Even if we designed the best parking lot—if we used permeable materials with vegetated swales and shaded it with trees and achieved a neutral impact on the site's ecosystems—we did not want a visitor's first experience of the site to be a parking lot."

GREG MELLA
SmithGroupJJR

61

Photo: Courtesy Hourigan Construction

Photo: Prakash Patel

A LIVING CONSTRUCTION SITE

Hourigan Construction was committed to protecting the site and minimizing other negative impacts during the construction of the Brock Environmental Center. While the Conservation and Reuse Imperative mandated that the project minimize construction waste, Hourigan went well beyond the minimum requirements.

"If we were going to build something that doesn't contribute negative effects to the environment—if we were going to minimize energy use, stay away from carbon-emitting systems and avoid Red List materials—we wanted to be sure to do the same thing during construction," says Chris Brandt, Executive Vice President of Hourigan Construction.

Here are some of the measures his company took during the construction of the Brock Center:

- Mobile photovoltaic arrays provided power during construction, accounting for about half of the energy used on the job

- To minimize lighting impact, site security lighting was set on motion detectors

- Workers parked off-site most of the time, except for delivery trucks

- In order to reduce carbon emissions, catalytic converters were outfitted on all excavators, generators, and forklifts

- To reduce equipment noise, filters and baffles were outfitted on all exhaust systems

- The project utilized on-site well water rather than chlorinated city water

- A "green construction trailer" was outfitted with high-efficiency HVAC units and glazing, and was built using reclaimed materials, including ceiling tiles

THE WATER PETAL

Pebble in the Pond

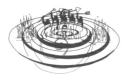

Photo: Chris Gorri

65

The Water Petals **PEBBLE IN THE POND**

SUMMARY OF THE LIVING BUILDING CHALLENGE VERSION 2.1 WATER PETAL

Petal Intent

The intent of the Water Petal is to realign how people use water and redefine "waste" in the built environment, so that water is respected as a precious resource. Scarcity of potable water is quickly becoming a serious issue as many countries around the world face severe shortages and compromised water quality. Even regions that have avoided the majority of these problems to date due to a historical presence of abundant fresh water are at risk: the impacts of climate change, highly unsustainable water use patterns, and the continued drawdown of major aquifers portend significant problems ahead.

Petal Imperatives

- Net Zero Water
- Ecological Water Flow

"The things people talk about most with regard to the Merrill Center are the water solutions—composting toilets and rainwater collection. You can't think about The Chesapeake Bay without thinking about water."

GREG MELLA
SmithGroupJJR

"The biggest challenge was designing a water collection and purification system that met all state and federal guidelines. Navigating the regulatory process was tedious and challenging given that it's not something I do every day, but in the end it was the most gratifying success to receive a public waterworks permit and drink the rainwater!"

BRIAN COFFIELD
SmithGroupJJR

IMPERATIVE:
NET ZERO WATER

IMPERATIVE:
ECOLOGICAL WATER FLOW

The Brock Environmental Center project was registered under Living Building Challenge 2.1. At that time, the Standard broke the Water Petal into two Imperatives: Net Zero Water, which stipulates that all water used in a project must come from captured precipitation, and Ecological Water Flow, which stipulates that all wastewater and stormwater must be managed on-site.

67

In actuality, a Living Building functions like an organism, and all of the systems that capture, transport, use, and treat water are integrated. This thinking is reflected in Living Building Challenge 3.0, which unified the Water Petal under a single Imperative.

Whether one Imperative or two, the Brock team faced both technical and regulatory challenges in meeting the Water Petal requirements.

When the Merrill Center was completed in Maryland in 2000, the project showcased pioneering approaches to water conservation. It was a public building that relied exclusively on composting toilets and that collected rainwater for all non-potable uses, plus hand washing, which the team later learned was considered a potable use. The Brock design team was surprised to learn that in the years since the Merrill Center had been completed, no other public project had accomplished as much. With the Brock Center, CBF wanted to raise the bar for water conservation yet again. The team knew that the most significant barrier would be earning regulatory permission to drink rainwater collected on-site. The project's unconventional approaches to managing stormwater—including the decision to relegate parking off the site—would also meet with considerable resistance.

SmithGroupJJR designed the rainwater system. WPL, under the guidance of civil engineer Walter Weeks and landscape architect Billy Almond, took the lead in the design of the greywater and stormwater strategies. The years-long process required persistence, patient education, and the cultivation of allies within regulatory agencies. Today, the Brock Center successfully demonstrates that a building can contribute to the regeneration of ecosystems. The building only uses water that it can capture from the immediate site; it produces no waste; it helps the landscape absorb rainwater during heavy storms, and it contributes to the recharging of groundwater.

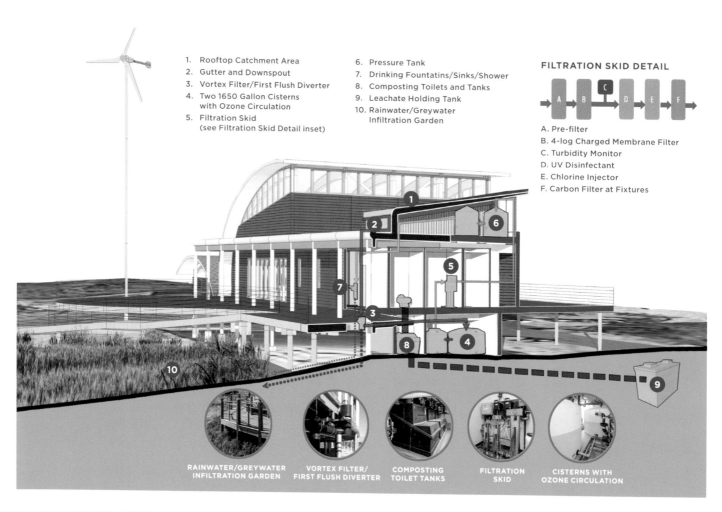

1. Rooftop Catchment Area
2. Gutter and Downspout
3. Vortex Filter/First Flush Diverter
4. Two 1650 Gallon Cisterns with Ozone Circulation
5. Filtration Skid (see Filtration Skid Detail inset)
6. Pressure Tank
7. Drinking Fountatins/Sinks/Shower
8. Composting Toilets and Tanks
9. Leachate Holding Tank
10. Rainwater/Greywater Infiltration Garden

FILTRATION SKID DETAIL

A. Pre-filter
B. 4-log Charged Membrane Filter
C. Turbidity Monitor
D. UV Disinfectant
E. Chlorine Injector
F. Carbon Filter at Fixtures

RAINWATER/GREYWATER INFILTRATION GARDEN

VORTEX FILTER/ FIRST FLUSH DIVERTER

COMPOSTING TOILET TANKS

FILTRATION SKID

CISTERNS WITH OZONE CIRCULATION

> *"Having been a regulator, you can easily get to the place where you think you can design a system better than the designer. They say, 'Why don't you just hook into the water line and make it easier on everybody?' If CBF hadn't had the backbone... I am proud that they took the initiative to get this system approved. They will be an important player as the regulations evolve, by having an informed opinion on the matter."*

NEIL WILLIAMS
Biohabitats

CAPTURING RAIN

The team's approach to the Water Petal mirrored its approach to the Energy Petal.

"We wanted to right size the system," says Greg Mella. "Smaller cisterns are less expensive than larger ones, and increasing efficiency decreases demand."

The team first focused on estimating the Brock Center's daily water demand and exploring ways to reduce that demand. While estimating demand for CBF's staff was relatively straightforward, doing so for thousands of potential visitors was trickier. SmithGroupJJR worked with CBF to estimate the number of visitors and predict how much they would use the facilities inside the Brock Center.

Next, the team focused on reducing demand. Right off the top, the choice to use composting toilets cut estimated water use by over two-thirds, saving nearly 50,000 gallons per year. Other strategies included specifying low-flow fixtures for lavatories and sinks and using recycled water for non-potable applications such as irrigation. After all of these strategies were factored in, the team estimated daily water demand for the Brock Center at a modest 145 gallons. This figure represents the combined use of all lavatories, mop sinks, water coolers, kitchen sinks, and showers.

SmithGroupJJR's engineers estimated water supply using rainfall data gathered from the Norfolk International Airport between August 1, 1948, and June 19, 2013. Unlike many regions in the country, there is no shortage of precipitation in Hampton Roads. Norfolk receives an average of 45 inches of rain per year, with little variation from month to month, and historic data shows that drought in Virginia Beach rarely lasts longer than three weeks. Consequently, the cisterns were sized to accommodate 3300 gallons—just over a three-week supply.

At the Merrill Center, dramatic and attractive wooden cisterns are showcased in prominent locations in front of the building, fulfilling CBF's goal of turning sustainable features into educational moments. To comply with the State of Virginia drinking water regulations, the cisterns used in the Brock Center's systems are made from polyethylene, meeting National Sanitation Foundation (NSF) requirements, and are located below the building in a mechanical room. Situating the tanks underneath the building enables a system that relies mostly on gravity to move water, which saves pumping energy and ensures the system can continue to operate during power outages. But it also means the cisterns are not highly visible, although tours of the building usually include a trip to the cistern and composting rooms. A single "pickle barrel" cistern next to the main entrance ramp and adjacent to the education pavilion sends a demonstrative message to visitors that rainwater collection is one of the Brock Center's important water strategies. The rainwater collected in this cistern provides irrigation water to new plantings in a nearby rain garden, along with teaching opportunities.

SUPPLY AND DEMAND

Estimated 3-week Water Use
3045 gallons

Actual Capacity of Cistern
3300 gallons

As with all of their building projects, CBF sought to highlight sustainable technologies in highly visible locations. Photo: Prakash Patel

BROCK ENVIRONMENTAL CENTER FOR A LIVING CHESAPEAKE

NAVIGATING THE PROCESS

While the team was challenged with designing a system that harvests and treats rainwater, the greater challenge was earning the regulatory permits that would allow CBF to use treated rainwater throughout the building for all uses, potable and non-potable. The Safe Drinking Water Act considers water collected from rooftops to be "surface water." Consequently, the permitting process and treatment requirements are the same as if it were being pumped from a creek or other natural source.

"On the one hand, regulators have a legitimate obligation to protect users of public water," says Neil Williams of Biohabitats, a firm hired by SmithGroupJJR to consult on the rainwater system. "But regulations never contemplated roof-top rainwater harvesting. This and the Waterworks requirement can be prohibitive."

A system that collects, stores, treats, and distributes high quality and safe (potable) water is considered a waterworks. Because it serves at least twenty-five people for at least six months out of the year, but not necessarily the same twenty-five people, the Brock Environmental Center is classified as a Transient Non-Community Waterworks. This classification mandates that a Class IV state-certified Waterworks Operator be on-site to oversee the system and conduct the required sampling and monitoring.

From prior experience at the Merrill Center, CBF and SmithGroupJJR understood the value of reaching out early to regulators and sought meetings with the permitting agencies involved, including the Virginia Department of Health - Office of Drinking Water (ODW). The team presented its proposed system to the ODW during a preliminary engineering conference on November 2012.

Those who were present at that first meeting describe the initial attitude of ODW officials as extremely reluctant. The team understood the agency's position. Charged with protecting public health and ensuring that drinking water is safe, public health officials are naturally cautious when approached with a novel design that lies outside the prescribed path. After this initial meeting, Paul Willey realized that CBF needed a champion— someone who would work with the permitting agencies regularly without being a nuisance—and he willingly took on this role.

"Their urgency for granting the permit wasn't our urgency," says Willey. "There was a willingness to consider our system, but at the same time they were very apprehensive because it was something that hadn't been done before."

Mella and Brian Coffield of SmithGroupJJR recognized that they were going to need help learning the vocabulary and navigating the permitting process, and so they sought the expertise of Pete Muñoz and Neil Williams from Biohabitats, a firm which specializes in conservation planning, ecological restoration, and regenerative design. Muñoz had been involved in other Living Building Challenge projects and ported valuable knowledge to the Brock project. Williams

71

"On the one hand, regulators have a legitimate obligation to protect users of public water. But regulations never contemplated roof-top rainwater harvesting. Roofs are considered surfaces, so they're stuck with the same regulations as if water was pumped out of a creek. I think there's a legitimate need to create best practices and inspections specifically for rooftops."

NEIL WILLIAMS
Biohabitats

"We got the permit the day of the dedication. They came to do the testing, and we're all there— the whole building is based on getting this permit. They do the test, and the guy's like, 'Okay.' And I said, 'Okay? Does that mean we get the permit?' He said, 'Yeah, you get it.' It was very anticlimactic."

PAUL WILLEY
Chesapeake Bay Foundation

"Some of the LBC teams have gotten worn down and given up on the Water Petal because they knew that once they got the rejection it was over. But we've seen so many of these barriers fall: we've seen net zero buildings; we've seen buildings that treat all of their own wastewater. The rainwater system was going to be one of those barriers for us. If we and CBF can't do it—we ought to be the ones! We weren't going to give up. We were going to keep pushing."

RUS PERRY
SmithGroupJJR

"I learned that we had to learn the vocabulary. We had to learn what a PER was; I had to accept that 'Waterworks' wasn't something off a Monopoly board. The Office of Drinking Water is very bureaucratic, maybe more so than other bureaucratic institutions. But once we learned the agency's language, we were able to make a lot more headway."

GREG MELLA
SmithGroupJJR

had regulatory experience, and later helped validate the third-party testing of the rainwater system's components.

The team had originally hoped to acquire the permit by the time they broke ground on the project, in August 2013. But the process took much longer.

In February of 2013, Dan Horne, Engineering Field Director for ODW, sent a letter stating that the system as proposed would not be accepted because it did not treat water to federal and state potable standards. He also expressed concerns about the cross-connections among city water, rainwater collection, and the Brock Center's potable water system.

In June 2013, SmithGroupJJR submitted the Preliminary Engineering Report for the rainwater collection, treatment and distribution system. The report described the roof material, vortex filter, and cistern design, and detailed the "treatment train," which consisted of a turbidity pre-filter, a membrane "ultra-filter" and UV light disinfection, but no chlorine disinfection.

In October, Horne finally replied with comments. First, the system as designed did not provide the disinfection method that meets the State's potable water standards, which rely on chlorination rather than UV disinfection and requires residual chlorine levels of at least 0.2 mg/L. Next, the filtration and disinfection equipment would have to be verified by a qualified third party. The proposal would have to address how the fire suppression system (fire sprinklers) would be supplied, and how it would be designed to prevent backflow. ODW also needed to be able to test the source water before it underwent filtration and disinfection; in particular, the agency was concerned that the rainwater might be too acidic, in which case it could potentially corrode pipes and equipment.

In February 2014, the team sent its revised design, which included chlorination as an additional and final step in the treatment process. This revised report also clarified that the fire sprinkler system would be connected to municipal water and would be totally separate from the rainwater system. At the same time, the team sent a formal appeal to the Office of Drinking Water, requesting that the agency approve the system without chlorination, as originally designed. Throughout this period, Willey acted as "squeaky wheel," regularly checking in with ODW on the application's progress.

72

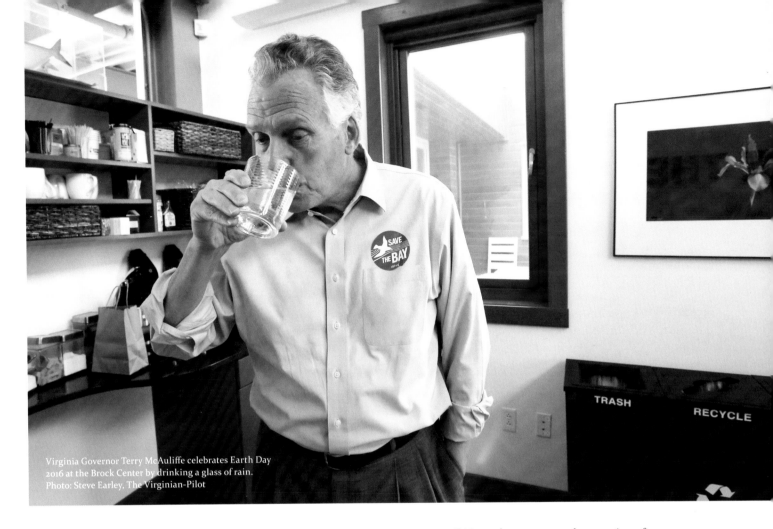

Virginia Governor Terry McAuliffe celebrates Earth Day 2016 at the Brock Center by drinking a glass of rain.
Photo: Steve Earley, The Virginian-Pilot

Meanwhile, CBF hired MSA, P.C., a firm which offers services in Land Planning, Surveying, Civil and Environmental Engineering, and Landscape Architecture, to conduct weekly sampling and inspections. MSA also services the treatment units and reports to ODW. But there was still the matter of having a Waterworks Operator on-site. Chris Gorri, who had served as Events Coordinator for the Merrill Center, had accepted the position of Building Operations Manager for the Brock Center. In addition to his other new duties, he agreed to take on the responsibility of becoming a Class IV Waterworks Operator. The training for his certification included a six-day class at Virginia Tech.

The team did not know for certain whether they would ultimately receive permission for the system as it was designed. If it was not approved, they would have had to compromise with a hybrid system that relied on treated rainwater for non-potable uses and municipal water for potable uses.

It was not until November 14, 2014—the morning of the Brock Center's official opening—that CBF received notification that its permit had been approved.

The team is proud of the fact that the system meets all requirements of the state and federal regulations.

"We met this thing to the letter of the law," says Mella. "Brock's system is a bona fide waterworks; there's not one variance." During the lengthy process of reviewing and approving the system, the Virginia Department of Health had become a true partner with CBF. ODW has brought other waterworks operators to tour the Brock Center, and a photo from an Earth Day celebration in April of 2016 captures a milestone.

73

AN ELEGANT SYSTEM

The Brock Center's waterworks starts with the sky. Rainwater is collected from 5,500 square feet of roof area, including the south-facing roof that includes the flush-mounted photovoltaic modules.

The vortex filter diverts the first flush of rain to a rain garden.

Although the Galvalume roofing material is not certified to NSF Standard 51, which governs potable water catchment areas, the team was able to provide documentation from the Texas Water Development Board. Specifically, the agency's Texas Manual on Rainwater Harvesting cites Galvalume as an acceptable surface from which to collect rainwater.

The 3:12 roof pitch is steep enough to ensure that dust and debris do not get trapped in the seams or pores; the slope also facilitates rinsing during the first flush of a rain event. Rainfall flows down the roof and into a continuous gutter; from there it funnels into one of two centrally-located downspouts. The gutters include leaf guards to minimize debris entering the water. To comply with the Red List and ensure the quality of the water, the solder used in both the gutters and downspouts is free of lead.

A vortex filter uses centrifugal action to direct the first flush of rain to a rain garden located right next to the south deck. After the first flush, rainwater flows into two 1,650-gallon cisterns located underneath the building. A pump circulates ozone through the cisterns to prevent algae growth. From there, water flows into the building and into a dedicated closet west of the lobby. In order to meet the strict requirements of both the EPA and the State of Virginia, the collected rainwater undergoes a series of treatments that reduce turbidity and disinfect the water. The first of these is a pre-filter, which removes particles from 25 microns down to 1 micron; from there it enters a pleated cartridge charged membrane filter, which removes particles down to 0.01 microns. Next, water undergoes UV disinfection before being treated with chlorine in the final step.

After chlorination, water is pumped into a loft above the closet and into a tank that contains calcium carbonate. This mineral increases the pH of the water so that it does not leach copper from distribution pipes. From there, water flows into a 300-gallon pressure tank, which provides water to the rest of the building at 45 to 50 psi. Carbon filters which remove the chlorine are provided in all drinking water fixtures at the point of use.

74

Two 1,650-gallon cisterns supply the Brock Center with all of its water, including drinking water. Photo: Dave Chance

SAFETY STANDARDS FOR POTABLE WATER

Turbidity:
95% of samples must measure less than
0.3 NTU (Nephelometric Turbidity Units)

Giardia lamblia:
99.9% inactive or removed

Viruses:
99.99% inactive or removed

Cryptosporidium:
99% inactive or removed

TESTING AND TROUBLESHOOTING

As the Brock Center's on-site Waterworks Operator, Chris Gorri works with Charles Hall and Edward "Dirk" Lynch of MSA, P.C. to manage the rainwater collection and treatment system. His duties include daily testing of the treated water's turbidity, residual chlorine, and temperature.

Being a Waterworks Operator means being observant to changes or potential problems. In June 2014, staff at the Brock Center started to notice a metallic taste in the water. The waterworks permit does not require CBF to test for metal, but Gorri asked MSA, P.C. if they could do so. Testing revealed slightly elevated levels of copper. Gorri immediately had his staff stop drinking the water until they could correct the problem. He also contacted the Office of Drinking Water right away.

Rainwater is typically clean and soft and has a low dissolved mineral content; as such, it can readily attract certain elements. As the rainwater flowed through the copper distribution pipes, it was dissolving copper into the water. CBF remedied the problem by adding calcium carbonate to the cisterns to harden the water; however,

this may have caused the expensive charged membrane filter to clog quickly. As an alternative solution, CBF added a treatment step after filtration. A calcium carbonate reactor tank next to the pressure tank now treats the water, raising the pH and hardness enough so that it does not attract copper from the distribution pipes.

"Now that we have the permit, when we have little issues, the first thing we do is call MSA and the health department," says Christy Everett. "Most of the time the health department officials say it's not a problem, but thanks for letting us know. The point is to keep that relationship open."

Gorri enjoys the challenge of maintaining a complex system, but even more, he enjoys sharing it with others.

"Telling guests of the center that they're drinking treated rainwater has been a great teaching tool and educational experience for all," says Gorri. "It has also been wonderful to share what we have learned with other organizations that are now working to implement systems like ours in their own projects."

"Three years ago, if you would had told me everything that I would now know about treating rainwater, I wouldn't have believed you. After this experience with just a 10,500 square foot building, I have a whole newfound respect for public works and the time and effort they put into providing water to an entire city. Operating the first commercial building permitted to do this had its challenges, especially when there wasn't a comparable system to use as a guide. I am fortunate to be surrounded by a team of brilliantly talented individuals who have taught me how to manage the system and solve issues if and when they arise."

CHRISTOPHER GORRI
Chesapeake Bay Foundation

"Every once in a while you come across the prospect to be involved with something great. The Brock Environmental Center is a flagship of sustainable possibilities that includes drinking water made from rainwater. MSA has been honored by the opportunity to assist the wonderful folks there and to operate and maintain this unique water system. Bottoms up!"

CHARLES HALL AND EDWARD "DIRK" LYNCH
MSA, P.C.

WASTE AS A RESOURCE

CBF had been using composting toilets for decades. Not only do the fixtures function beautifully, they conserve thousands of gallons of water. Having proven that composting toilets are practical even for a large, busy public building in Annapolis was crucial for convincing officials that they would also work in Virginia.

Based on previous experience, CBF knew that the composting toilets would yield two different products: the composted solids, and excess liquid wastewater, known as leachate, that drains from the composter units. CBF planned to dispose of the composted solids on-site, but the issue of leachate was more nuanced. At the Merrill Center, leachate is routed into the city sewer system, but that was not an option for the Brock Center.

"We looked at urine separation systems, such as urine diverting toilets, and considered the merits of diluting and applying the urine on-site," says Mella. "But this didn't feel like a solution that celebrated the notion that waste equals food." In addition, applying excess nutrients to a flood-prone site could contribute to water quality issues for the Bay.

CBF connected the team with Charles Bott, the progressive Director of Water Technology and Research at the Hampton Roads Sanitation District, and through him learned about struvite reactors. Made by reacting urine with a precipitate, struvite is a commercial-grade fertilizer that slowly releases phosphorus, nitrogen, and magnesium. The team considered producing the struvite on-site, but small, building-scale struvite reactors do not exist. Then they learned that Nansemond, a wastewater treatment facility five miles from Pleasure House Point, was already making the product.

The team also decided that on-site application of the struvite was not a good idea. The native marsh plants thrive in nutrient-poor conditions, and so did not require supplemental fertilizers.

77

Composter bins located underneath the building receive solids and liquids from all of the building's toilets. Photo: Dave Chance

78

Overfertilizing plants in a floodplain could lead to excess nutrients running off into the adjacent creeks, possibly causing eutrophication. CBF took advantage of scale jumping, which allows Living Building Challenge teams to consider solutions beyond the individual building or project scale, and delivers the leachate to the Nansemond facility four times a year. This way, the Center's leachate is converted into fertilizer that can be applied to plants in other locations that actually need the nutrients.

The composting toilets funnel effluent into five composter units, which are located in a concrete room underneath the building. The positioning of the bins was considered very carefully. Because the building is elevated, the team was able to take advantage of gravity. However, locating the bins so close to grade brought up other concerns; namely, the possibility of contamination during storm surges. To ward against this possibility, the vault was designed to

withstand wave action. It was also designed with a thirty-inch threshold at the entry, and the bins themselves are elevated and braced. A sump pump system was also installed, in case flood waters ever enter the composting tank room.

The material in the composters must be turned several times each month. A rich humus will be harvested from the bins every year and buried on-site, in compliance with local health department regulations, which do not allow surface application of "humanure."

At 1,300 gallons, the leachate tank is sized to hold up to six months' worth of leachate. The building management system includes alarms programmed to sound if the leachate tank is becoming full, and/or if the leachate tank overflows into the city sewer system. So far, this alarm has never sounded.

BIOSWALE PERMEABLE PAVER DRIVE RAINWATER RUNOFF BIOSWALE PERMEABLE PAVER WALK

SITE STRATEGIES

Earning approval for its treatment of stormwater and greywater proved almost as challenging as earning the waterworks permit. The Brock Center project proposed several unconventional site strategies, several of which were unprecedented in the City of Virginia Beach:

- Off-site parking on two public right-of ways (Winston Place and Marlin Bay Drive)

- Parking areas, road, and walkway consisting of permeable pavers with perimeter rain gardens as stormwater strategy

- On-site treatment for overflow rainwater in rain gardens

- A permeable gravel road that would provide emergency access

- On-site treatment of greywater

The first four approaches had to be approved by the City of Virginia Beach Department of Public Works; the greywater strategy required approval from the Virginia Department of Public Health. All of these approaches were detailed on the site plan, which was submitted to the City for approval. Once submitted, multiple departments, each with its own standards, reviewed the site plan. Several of these items did not fall within the City's standards. Fortunately, the team found an ally in Barry Frankenfield who, at the time, was director of Virginia Beach's Strategic Growth Area Office. Billy Almond and Walter Weeks of WPL Site Design attended several meetings, explaining the project goals and how individual items would function. They worked the design through several iterations before it was finally approved by the City in July 2013.

The Brock Center produces greywater, or used water, from sinks, showers, and drinking fountains. In Virginia, greywater is considered sewage, and its on-site use is

"City standards are very restrictive. CBF was building a pervious street in a public right of way, and the City Engineer in Public Works Department didn't want a new system to take care of. The other issue was that code requires a certain amount of parking on-site. It was difficult for people to understand the concept of such limited parking. What I had to do was carry this concept of Low Impact Development—which includes pervious pavers, minimal parking, and minimal street width—for CBF and the city manager, who was very supportive, and on down. When someone resisted these concepts and said no, I would say, 'that's the wrong answer.'"

BARRY FRANKENFIELD
City of Virginia Beach

"Discussing the site and stormwater design with the City in the early stages was vital in getting the design approved in a reasonable time frame."

WALTER WEEKS
WPL Site Design

"Earning approval to use new systems that are not part of the City of Virginia Beach manual on allowed paving systems meant we were not only breaking new ground here, but changing city standards, allowing the City of Virginia Beach to use more sustainable paving sections within the city. And then maybe the adjacent cities will adopt these new standards and presto—you are not just creating twelve sustainable parking spaces; you are transforming city standards and encouraging the adoption of better ideas across the city, state, and nation."

GREG MELLA
SmithGroupJJR

80

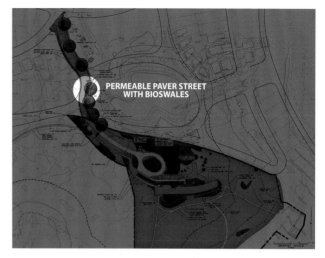

PERMEABLE PAVER STREET WITH BIOSWALES

GREYWATER INFILTRATION BASIN

RAIN GARDEN

Shown here in early spring, the "greywater dune" treats all used water from the building.
Photo: Billy Almond

governed by the Commonwealth of Virginia Sewage Handling and Disposal Regulations. Among other requirements, these regulations stipulate that:

- Greywater must be discharged at least 24" above groundwater

- Greywater must be discharged at least 18" below grade (no surface application)

- Greywater cannot be stored for more than 48 hours

- Emergency overflow to city sanitary sewer must be provided

At the Brock Center, greywater is collected in an underground tank beneath the building, just outside the composting tank room. The tank was sized to accommodate two and a half days' worth of greywater, or 468 gallons, and it includes emergency overflow to the City sanitary sewer. The tank is also outfitted with an alarm that sounds when the water reaches a prescribed level.

Effluent from the tank is pumped daily to a raised infiltration basin. Because the site is in a floodplain, and the water table is high, WPL designed the infiltration basin to resemble a raised dune. This way, it meets the requirement for separation from groundwater and the requirement to discharge greywater at

least 18 inches below grade, while also blending in with the native environment. The dune was planted with Juncus grass.

WPL worked with CBF to minimize impervious surfaces on the site, and the final design resulted in just 8 percent impervious cover; however, all run-off is either captured in cisterns or infiltrated into the ground. This is how, even though the site has been developed with a building, roads, and other infrastructure, it does not contribute any runoff to surrounding waterways.

There are no concrete or asphalt paved surfaces on the site. The staff parking area on Winston Place, the walkway leading to the building, and the ADA parking spaces next to the building are comprised of permeable pavers installed above an aggregate base. This was an alternative to the typical system, which consists of paved surfaces and pipes that direct stormwater to an infiltration basin.

The Winston Place parking area was the first permeable paver section in a public street to receive stormwater credit and to be approved by the City of Virginia Beach. The Holland Stone pavers with half-inch joints used in the installation meet ICPI (Interlocking Concrete Pavement Institute) standards, meaning they are strong enough to withstand pedestrian and vehicular traffic, but enable 100 percent surface permeability.

81

The staff parking area, ADA parking spaces and walkway utilize a permeable paver system that allows stormwater to infiltrate. Photo: Tim Solanic

"This was a game-changing project. I don't think CBF realizes how far the tentacles have reached in the developed world. It has even changed the way our engineers approach projects. I don't know how many times I've said, 'Well, we did that at Brock, so why not here?'"

BILLY ALMOND
WPL Site Design

"This was pioneering," says Billy Almond of WPL Site Design. "There is nothing in the public works standards that allows for this." WPL is working on similar installations for other projects within the City of Virginia Beach.

Because the region experiences extreme rain events—for example, one six-week period in 2016 saw three intense storms that yielded 46 inches of rain—WPL included linear rain gardens lining the permeable paver walkway. These rain gardens provide extra insurance during heavy storms, capturing any overflow from the parking area and walkway.

Several rain gardens around the building treat first flush stormwater and rainwater from roofs that do not drain into the collection cisterns. These areas have been planted with native plants that can withstand a range of moisture conditions. Other native plants have voluntarily seeded and are filling in these gardens, as well.

STORMWATER STRATEGIES

- Permeable paver parking area, walkway, and ADA parking spaces

- Rain gardens along the permeable paver walkway and around building treat stormwater from walkway during high rain events; runoff from roofs and excess rainwater flows to rain gardens once cisterns are full

- Greywater infiltration basin (dune)

- Gravel access road, fire lane, and turnaround

- Naturalized landscape with no turf areas

Rain gardens line the permeable walkway and driveway. Photo: Chris Gorri

83

THE ENERGY PETAL

Powerful Strategies

Photo: Prakash Patel

The Energy Petal: **POWERFUL STRATEGIES**

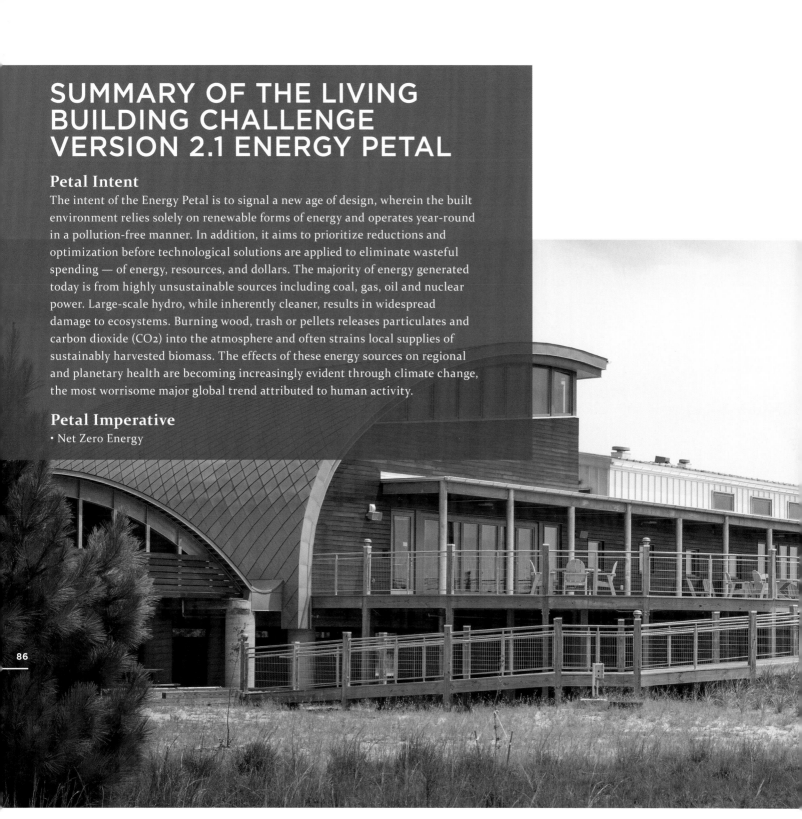

SUMMARY OF THE LIVING BUILDING CHALLENGE VERSION 2.1 ENERGY PETAL

Petal Intent

The intent of the Energy Petal is to signal a new age of design, wherein the built environment relies solely on renewable forms of energy and operates year-round in a pollution-free manner. In addition, it aims to prioritize reductions and optimization before technological solutions are applied to eliminate wasteful spending — of energy, resources, and dollars. The majority of energy generated today is from highly unsustainable sources including coal, gas, oil and nuclear power. Large-scale hydro, while inherently cleaner, results in widespread damage to ecosystems. Burning wood, trash or pellets releases particulates and carbon dioxide (CO_2) into the atmosphere and often strains local supplies of sustainably harvested biomass. The effects of these energy sources on regional and planetary health are becoming increasingly evident through climate change, the most worrisome major global trend attributed to human activity.

Petal Imperative

• Net Zero Energy

Getting to net zero energy required lowering energy demand by 80 percent. Photo: Scott Wertz

IMPERATIVE:
NET ZERO ENERGY

Technically, CBF had built low energy-use buildings before: their off-the-grid education centers in remote locations around The Chesapeake Bay, and the Merrill Center, which relies in part on solar energy. However, designing a large, very busy environmental education center that met the single Imperative of the Energy Petal was an endeavor on a different scale. The Brock Environmental Center needed to generate at least as much energy as it consumed, while accommodating office activity, school programs, and conferences all year round.

The design team's approach to achieving the Energy Petal followed what Greg Mella likes to call "the holy trinity": reduce demand using passive strategies; meet the resulting demand with efficient systems; and supply those efficient systems with renewable energy.

Mella and engineer Cindy Cogil brought many of the lessons learned from the Merrill Center to this new project. The design team planned to optimize the strategies that had worked well; in particular, natural ventilation and geothermal-based HVAC. The many operable windows enabled extensive use of natural ventilation at the Merrill Center, and the windows are used for cooling more often than had been predicted. The ground source heat pump system, which is connected to a geothermal well field and provides both space heating and cooling, has also performed well, and furthermore, the team intended to incorporate a geothermal system into the Brock Center's HVAC system.

The Brock Center also gave the team an opportunity to learn from mistakes. Due to the many windows, the Merrill Center experienced problems with excessive passive solar gain and glare. The solar PV array on the Merrill Center also did not perform optimally because the modules were used as sun shades and were themselves frequently shaded.

87

THE IMPORTANCE OF MODELING

The approach to high-performance buildings had evolved in the fifteen years since the Merrill Center was designed and built. Building codes had raised standards for R-values of walls and roofs, and the design team also had access to sophisticated energy modeling tools that were not available during the design of the Merrill Center.

SmithGroupJJR took full advantage of these tools and used extensive energy modeling to optimize the building's performance and meet the needs of the client. The design team used simulation to test many "design moves" early in the process. This simulation included modeling building orientation, building depth, window layouts, daylighting, and envelope characteristics. Later, Baumann Consulting developed a predictive energy model which estimated the building's annual energy use. This comprehensive model took into account the building envelope, the program schedule, plug loads, lighting, the HVAC system, and the number of hours cooling loads could be met using natural ventilation. Baumann refined the model as SmithGroupJJR finalized various aspects of the design. Individual studies of the envelope, HVAC system, daylighting and airflows helped inform the model and make it as accurate as possible.

Cindy Cogil was involved in this effort initially; once she accepted a new position with SmithGroupJJR, she handed the reins to Brian Coffield, who served as lead engineer for the duration of the project. Greg, Brian, and electrical engineer Sara Lappano worked closely together throughout the design period.

The configuration of the windows exemplifies how SmithGroupJJR used an integrated design process to arrive at the best solutions for the Brock Center. The number and locations of windows, the use of exterior awnings, and the windows' R-values and type of glazing affect many features and functions of the building, including the quality and effectiveness of daylighting, natural ventilation, the energy efficiency of the building's envelope, and its aesthetics. Close collaboration and detailed modeling helped to balance all of these factors to not only yield the most energy benefits, but to optimize occupant comfort and enhance the building's connection with the outdoors.

AN IMPRESSIVE EUI

During the design charrette, SmithGroupJJR had identified a target Energy Use Intensity, or EUI, of 20 for the Brock Environmental Center. This metric measures a building's energy use per square foot per year, and is calculated by dividing a building's total annual energy use (in kBtus) by its gross floor area. Though higher than some of the Living Building Challenge projects the team had studied, Mella felt it was a realistic target, given the challenging hot-humid climate and the likelihood that the building would be used seven days a week.

As the predictive model developed, the EUI was progressively lowered. Once the HVAC system and contribution of natural ventilation were factored into the model, the EUI was lowered to 17; a later refinement of the model predicted an EUI of 15.85—more than 80 percent lower than similar commercial buildings in the region. The building's actual EUI, based on its first full year of monitoring, was an impressive 14.14.

BRINGING IN THE CLIENT

One of the truths about high-performance buildings is that, as heating and cooling loads diminish, other loads such as lighting and plug loads become larger pieces of the energy pie. Consequently, it was important to involve the client at a deeper level to try to predict what those loads might be—and to try to reduce them.

While energy modeling is common for projects pursuing LEED certification or other energy-performance goals, these models are typically based on cost comparisons and often utilize generic values for certain categories. The team members knew they needed a highly accurate predictive model to achieve the goal of net zero energy. Instead of assigning generic values, they worked with Mary Tod Winchester, Paul Willey, and Chris Gorri of CBF to obtain detailed information about how they were going to use the building, from estimated thermostat settings to how many weekends they thought they might rent the facility, to the kind of equipment they would be using. Ultimately, they were able to create a daily operational schedule for each space, down to the hour. The design team also worked with CBF to help them choose office equipment, finishes, and furniture that would impact energy use and daylighting.

"I've never worked on a project where we had to understand in detail how the owner was going to use and occupy a building at this level so early in the process. That is something we should be doing. We create buildings so owners can use them effectively. These conversations are a little unusual now, but will become the norm in the future."

GREG MELLA
SmithGroupJJR

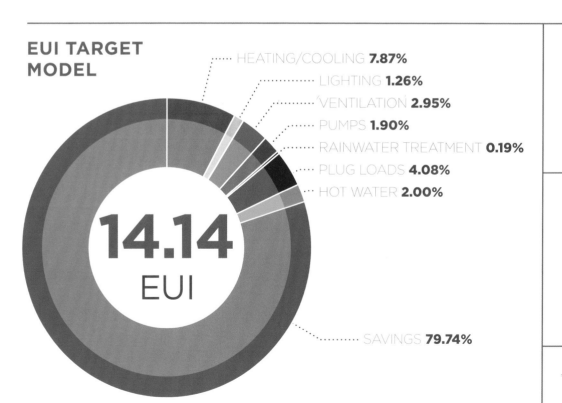

EUI TARGET MODEL

HEATING/COOLING **7.87%**
LIGHTING **1.26%**
VENTILATION **2.95%**
PUMPS **1.90%**
RAINWATER TREATMENT **0.19%**
PLUG LOADS **4.08%**
HOT WATER **2.00%**

14.14 EUI

SAVINGS **79.74%**

80%
SAVINGS FROM BASELINE

69.82
KBTU/SF/YEAR BASELINE EUI*

* ASHRAE 90.1 – 2007,
  Medium Office category, all climates

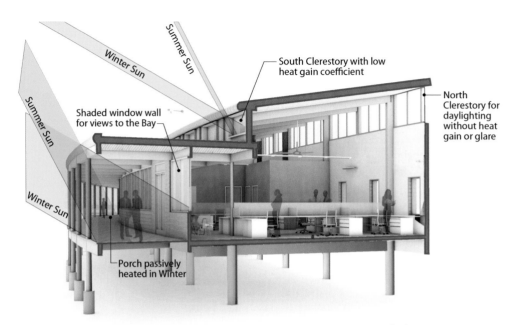

Preventing unwanted solar gain was an important part of the Brock Center's energy strategy.

ENVELOPE STRATEGIES

One of SmithGroupJJR's first in-house modeling studies explored the energy implications of both the building orientation and the degree of the building's curve.

Not surprisingly, aligning the building directly on the east-west axis yielded the most energy benefits. Increasing the radius of the curve showed improvements in energy intensity, as the curve enabled the solar array to capture early morning light from the southeast. However, increasing the radius also increased the total square footage of the building, and thus its overall energy use. The team modified the design to both retain the curve without increasing the square footage.

Another one of SmithGroupJJR's initial strategies for "getting to zero" was to optimize the building envelope and reduce heating and cooling demand. Baumann Consulting developed optimization curves for various R-values. Greg Mella initially anticipated that, for the climate, with its hot, humid summers and mostly mild winters, the "sweet spot" values for the walls and roof would be R-25 and R-30, respectively. However, simulations suggested compelling benefits from much higher values. It was a good lesson about the value of simulation tools over "rule-of-thumb" thinking.

"We have the worst of both worlds in Virginia Beach," says Mella. "It gets really hot in summer, but it also gets really cold in winter, and envelope improvements are about reducing thermal loads."

The R-35 walls consist of 2 x 6 wood framing, the cavities of which are filled with 5 1/2 inches of high-density batt insulation. A fluid-applied membrane on the exterior plywood sheathing provides an effective permeable air barrier. Three inches of rigid extruded polystyrene (XPS) insulation are installed against the sheathing. A rainscreen assembly, made from furring strips of the same reclaimed cypress that forms the cladding, addresses moisture infiltration in the storm-prone environment.

The R-50 roof assembly consists of vented composite panels, which are comprised of half-inch plywood, a one-inch air space, and 8 1/2 inches of polyisocyanurate insulation. A vapor-permeable self-adhering underlayment is installed to the exterior of these panels, and standing-seam Galvalume roofing is installed on top of the underlayment. The elevated foundation is insulated with five inches of XPS insulation and achieves an insulation value of R-31. The building essentially functions as an insulated box atop a concrete plinth.

When choosing the optimal window package, SmithGroupJJR considered several factors: the overall glazing ratio, the role of exterior shading, window styles, and the R-value of the windows—specifically, the benefits of triple glazing and different high-performance glass options.

SmithGroupJJR had learned a hard lesson from the Merrill Center: there is such a thing as too much glass. With a glazing ratio on the south façade of over 50 percent, the building suffers from overheating and glare. Early modeling studies for the Brock Center identified an ideal window-to-wall ratio of around 20-30 percent. In addition, preliminary energy models showed that enhancing the Brock Center's envelope would preclude the need for additional passive solar heating in winter. (The winter climate, characterized by temperatures that frequently fluctuate, also made passive solar heating in winter somewhat unpredictable, and at times, undesirable.) With this in mind, the team designed awnings and overhangs that allow outdoor spaces, including the long porch on the south façade, to be bathed in sunlight during winter, while blocking direct sunlight to interior spaces in both summer and winter.

The triple-paned, argon-filled windows from Intus Windows have an R-value of 6.67 (u = 0.15). As with the walls and roof, modeling showed a significant benefit to specifying windows with R-values well above what the team had anticipated. Though the simulations showed additional benefits to going as high as R-9, these benefits had to be balanced with the increasing costs.

WALL OPTIMIZATION STUDY

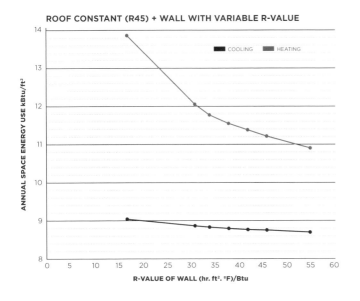

ROOF CONSTANT (R45) + WALL WITH VARIABLE R-VALUE

ROOF OPTIMIZATION STUDY

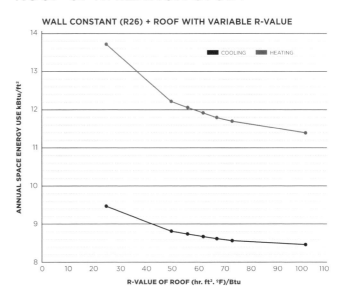

WALL CONSTANT (R26) + ROOF WITH VARIABLE R-VALUE

"When you draw window elevations, you include a symbol to indicate which side has a hinge and how the window opens. I have never in my career thought about where and how I draw that symbol. But for this project we had to think about not just what kind of window or how big the window is or where it was located, but even how it functions and where the hinges are located."

GREG MELLA
SmithGroupJJR

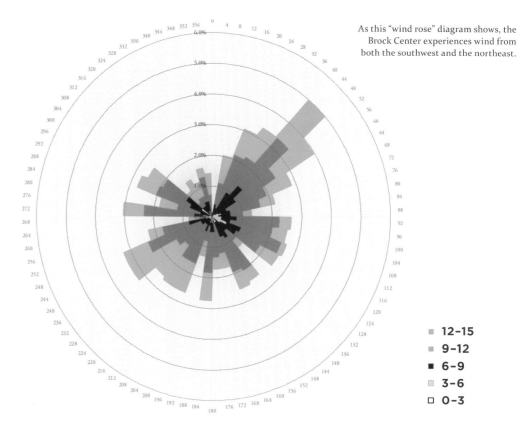

As this "wind rose" diagram shows, the Brock Center experiences wind from both the southwest and the northeast.

12–15
9–12
6–9
3–6
0–3

WORKING WITH WIND

The success of natural ventilation had exceeded expectations at the Merrill Center, and was also an important strategy for the Brock Center. The two buildings posed different challenges.

The two-story Merrill Center experienced vertical stratification, and it was challenging to obtain good airflow inside the building. By contrast, the long, narrow single-story form of the Brock Center was more likely to create horizontal stratification.

The design team incorporated a dogtrot, or breezeway, into the building to enhance the connection with the outdoors. The dogtrot is a regional archetype that effectively funnels cooling breezes into interior spaces. It was used extensively in residential architecture in the Southeastern United States before the advent of mechanical air conditioning, and typically divided the public and private parts of the house. In the Brock Center, the dogtrot effectively breaks up the long form of the building. A wall of windows opens out onto The Chesapeake Bay, creating more

outdoor space, and while its other benefits are more difficult to quantify, it helps alleviate horizontal stratification, too.

Once the team optimized window locations for daylighting and aligned them with the siting energy model, they analyzed the "wind rose," which shows the frequency of winds blowing from particular directions. Unlike the Merrill Center site, which enjoys consistent breezes from the southeast, the Pleasure House Point site is characterized by bidirectional winds, which vary depending on time of day and time of year. Consequently, the design needed to be more flexible in order to capture winds from two directions. Breezes from the southwest funnel through the dogtrot windows and up through the north clerestory, while breezes from the northeast flow through the north windows and out through the south clerestory.

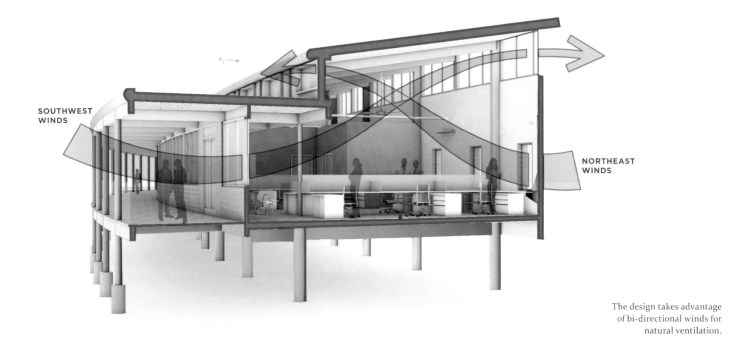

SOUTHWEST
WINDS

NORTHEAST
WINDS

The design takes advantage
of bi-directional winds for
natural ventilation.

To quantify the potential for natural ventilation, the design team worked with Baumann Consulting to build a model which focused on the office section of the building. The modeling team used the wind data from nearby Norfolk International Airport to isolate the number of hours per year that achieved a certain wind speed. Taking into account energy load profiles, solar gain, temperature and humidity, the model then predicted how many hours out of the year natural ventilation would be able to meet the loads. However, that number might be on the conservative side. The model did not take night flushing into account, nor did it factor in the benefits of the dogtrot. It also did not consider occupant behavior, which may be the biggest variable of all.

Coffield plotted temperature and relative humidity on a graph and compared it against ASHRAE 55, which is a standard for thermal comfort, in order to estimate how many hours per year natural ventilation might be possible. The real value of this graph was to show CBF how expanding the "comfort range" by a few degrees in either direction could increase the number of hours potentially available for natural ventilation.

Ultimately, the effectiveness of a natural ventilation design depends heavily on the user. High wind velocity at desk level, for instance, can cause discomfort and disrupt items. Windows may be shut in this case, even though that means losing the opportunity for natural ventilation. Mella and CBF had also learned from the Merrill Center that perception heavily influences occupant comfort. For instance, all other factors being equal, people feel colder on grey, cloudy days. Similarly, CBF staff are more tolerant of both lower and higher temperatures if the windows are open and they can experience a connection with the outdoors.

All windows at the Brock Center were designed to be opened manually, except for the south-facing clerestory windows. These windows are mechanically controlled, and are programmed to provide night flushing when temperature and humidity conditions are met.

93

"My favorite feature of the building is the natural ventilation system. It was my first experience having a client challenge me to do something outside of the box for cooling their building! At this site, natural ventilation really enhances the connection with the outdoors and has turned out to be a very effective cooling strategy for the occupants."

BRIAN COFFIELD
SmithGroupJJR

DAYLIGHTING

SmithGroupJJR designed the Brock Environmental Center with daylighting in mind. Its long, narrow form ensures natural light will penetrate most of the space, and the open plan includes few interior partitions that would block sunlight. The windows and clerestory on the north side of the building bring in ample amounts of diffuse light, and the south windows are shaded by a porch that blocks direct sunlight. All of these passive strategies reduce the demand for artificial, or electric lighting.

A more traditional approach to lighting creates uniform light levels in an office environment. But Sara Lappano worked with the interior design team, led by Cheryl Brown, to understand how office furniture was going to be arranged. This information allowed her to fine-tune the design so that the light levels above workstations are more intense than the areas in between. Work stations are arranged perpendicular to the window wall, and the design is flexible enough so that new stations can be added and still have adequate light levels.

The ceilings in the office area are quite high, so it was important to make sure light was not solely directed downward, but also upwards, where it could reflect off the white ceiling surface to create an even ambient illumination for the entire space. At that time, LED technology was on the cusp of viability and affordability. While fluorescent pendant fixtures emit light in all directions, LEDs provide more focused light. A design utilizing LEDs would have required both up-directed and down-directed lamps —twice as many units as Lappano ultimately specified. She sourced linear pendant fluorescent fixtures through Axis Lighting (the low-mercury fluorescent lamps required a Red List exception) and specified LED fixtures for downlights and task lighting elsewhere.

In the Merrill Center, there was a big emphasis on minimizing paints and finishes and using materials in their raw states— for example, unfinished oriented strand board (OSB) serves as the finished ceiling. However, the team learned that light surfaces—whether white-painted ceilings or light-colored desk tops—significantly enhance both electric lighting and daylighting. Here again, SmithGroupJJR worked with Brown and her team on material choices, including furniture, in order to optimize the lighting design. Lappano set a target of 20 footcandles (fc) for the office areas, which is below the average illumination for such spaces.

"We designed light levels on the lower end," says Lappano. "But we could get away with a little less light because we used a strategy that combined ambient and task lighting." The baseline light levels are adequate for most office functions, while individual desk lights provide brighter light for specific tasks, such as reading text.

94

Photo: Prakash Patel

Photo: Scott Wertz

LIGHTING CONTROLS AND PLUG LOADS

Lappano also designed a comprehensive lighting control system for the Brock Center.

"Even if we designed great daylighting strategy, you only get the energy benefit if you control when artificial lighting is used," says Lappano.

The system includes dimmable lights and occupancy sensors. The dimmable lights utilize photosensors that detect changing levels of daylight and dim up or down accordingly. In typical systems, such lights cannot dim below 10 percent. But in consulting with CBF, Lappano learned that even this low level of artificial illumination is often not necessary, and that daylighting could meet all of their needs on nearly all days. Therefore, Lappano changed the programming so that the lighting in the office area is turned off completely during daylight hours, saving a significant amount of energy.

Occupancy sensors direct lights to turn on or off in the presence or absence of people in the building. In the Brock Center, this strategy is not limited to lighting, but extends to plug loads as well. A control system powers off most of the receptacles in the building

at night. If someone enters the building after hours or on the weekend, he or she can override the system and return power to the receptacles. This strategy minimizes "vampire loads"—the energy that electronic equipment consumes when not in use but still plugged into receptacles. In residential buildings, vampire loads can account for up to 10 percent of equipment's energy use. That percentage is likely as high or higher in an office building with lots of electronic equipment.

The two exceptions are the IT rack and the refrigerator in the staff kitchen, which are always powered on. The refrigerator in the catering kitchen, on the other hand, can be turned on and off via a toggle switch on the wall; by default, it is left off until needed.

"CBF was willing to be really aggressive," says Lappano.

CBF's proactive approach extends to their choice of computers and copy machines. Office equipment uses between one quarter to one third of a building's energy and is highly variable in its energy efficiency. Lappano worked up some comparison scenarios for CBF so that they would understand how various choices affected energy use. For example, desk top computers with monitors consume much more energy than do laptop computers. These exercises helped CBF develop an "energy budget" and aided their selections, which included Energy Star-certified equipment.

A similar strategy of using lights only when needed extends outside the building. Lighting for the path through the forest is programmed to turn on in the evening for a discrete period of time, as staff are leaving for the night; the lights can also be turned on manually when needed. The lighting for the staff parking lot on Winston Place is technically within the jurisdiction of the City of Virginia Beach; however, SmithGroupJJR and CBF worked with the City to select the "greenest" fixtures that still met the City's requirements for illuminance.

AN INNOVATIVE HVAC SYSTEM

Coastal sites are often ideal for geothermal heat transfer.

The water table is high, and ground temperatures remain fairly constant. When the Merrill Center was built, geothermal systems were not widely used for commercial applications; however, CBF was willing to demonstrate innovative systems and agreed to take the risk. The system has performed so well that CBF and SmithGroupJJR agreed to incorporate one into the Brock Center's HVAC system.

In summer 2012, once the basic form, square footage, and functional spaces of the Brock Environmental Center had been determined, SmithGroupJJR embarked on a study to compare two HVAC options, both of which incorporated a vertical, closed loop geothermal well field to provide the heat rejection for building loads. The first system, which had been employed in the Merrill Center, utilized ground source heat pumps piped to the geothermal loops. The second alternative was a variable refrigerant flow (VRF) system that utilized one or more variable speed compressors to provide the heat rejection for building loads, connected to multiple indoor evaporator units.

In a VRF system, the compressor speed can change in order to deliver only the minimum amount of thermal energy that is needed at a given time. This feature enables control of individual zones, simultaneous heating and cooling, and heat exchange from one zone to another. Because the compressor speed modulates according to demand, it is more energy-efficient than a ground-source heat pump system.

The study ranked the two alternatives on several criteria: energy consumption, system maintainability, acoustics, controllability, aesthetics, and first cost. The VRF system edged out the heat pump system in all categories except for first cost. Most importantly, it lowered energy consumption by 5 percent, which reduced the size—and hence, the cost—of the renewable energy system required. (In other words, when the team factored in the cost of the photovoltaic modules "saved" due to its efficiency, the VRF system contributed to lower whole-building first costs.) A VRF system allows for more space control by allowing more zones, and it is more compatible with natural ventilation, as some zones can receive conditioned air while others are cooled with natural ventilation. The VRF system won out in aesthetics, too, as it requires less exposed ductwork. The system is also quiet.

After touring a site that includes a VRF installation, CBF once again agreed to take on the risk of demonstrating innovation and selected the ground-source VRF system.

The Brock Center's geothermal well field is located underneath the emergency fire lane to the north of the building, and consists of eighteen vertical wells that are 250 feet deep. A vertical well field was chosen to minimize disturbance to the site. The system provides forty tons of heating and cooling capacity and uses water only. (Many geothermal systems use a solution that includes glycol for freeze protection.)

The VRF system includes three indoor compressor units and eighteen indoor evaporator units. The indoor units vary in configuration in order to accommodate the demand from individual rooms. The system can provide both simultaneous heating and cooling to different zones and can provide heat recovery from one zone to another. The geothermal loops are also connected to the water-cooled dedicated outside air system, which provides the required ventilation air.

97

Photo: Courtesy Hourigan Construction

DEMONSTRATING RENEWABLE ENERGY

Solar power was not used optimally at the Merrill Center. Relative to today's standards, module efficiency was not as high, and the technology was very expensive. The location of the panels was chosen as much for their visibility to visitors as their performance, and the array ended up being shaded by the building part of the time. For the Brock Center, solar energy was a significantly more viable option for supplying a good portion of the building's power.

In keeping with the organization's strategy of using buildings as teaching tools, CBF wanted to incorporate renewable energy into the project, not only to meet the net zero energy goal, but to educate visitors about different technologies. In addition, diverse systems are inherently more resilient. Yet it was not until the green charrette and the initial site visit that the team was prompted to consider wind power as part of the renewable energy strategy. They decided to aim for a balance that would provide two-thirds of the energy from solar power and one-third from wind generation. Sun is more predictable than wind, and the team members felt more confident about estimating energy generation from solar power. They also decided to add a 10 percent "cushion" beyond the annual energy consumption calculated by the predictive energy model in case either renewable energy source underperformed.

One of the issues CBF and SmithGroupJJR had to confront was the potential impact of wind turbines on wildlife, and birds in particular. The site is in a bird migration route known as the Atlantic Flyway. Mary Tod Winchester talked with other organizations in the area that had installed turbines and that had conducted studies on bird mortality, and concluded that the impacts would be minimal. Still, she knew CBF would field many questions about their decision.

"Many environmental NGOs have chosen not to step into this discussion, choosing to avoid controversy," says Russell Perry of SmithGroupJJR. "The Chesapeake Bay Foundation researched the issue and concluded that small scale turbines reduced mortality to an acceptable rate, making them a preferable technology with the promise of helping to solve the atmospheric carbon imbalance."

While studying the mortality problem, Greg Mella and Sara Lappano learned that the kinetics—the spinning turbine blades—do not pose as much of a problem as does the physical obstruction of the tower. With that in mind, they decided that fewer, more efficient turbines would be a better choice than a "field" of many

98

Predictive Energy Model:
156 mmbtu/year

Target EUI:
18.9 kbtu/sq ft/year

Target on-site generation:
189 mmbtu

**Output Target
from Renewables:**
208 mmbtu/year

turbines. Mella liked the vertical axis turbines for their aesthetics, but as a whole they did not show strong performance. Instead, he and Lappano chose two horizontal-axis Excel 10 kW turbines from American manufacturer Bergey. In a volatile industry that saw many new companies coming and going each year, it was important to choose a product with verified performance. At the time, the Bergey model was the only small-scale turbine that was certified by the Small Wind Certification Council (SWCC). The combined production of the turbines represented approximately 30 percent of the total anticipated renewable energy production.

The design team also had to consider the effect of ground drag and turbulence on the turbines' performance. Turbulence is caused by objects on the earth, including trees and buildings. These objects create chaotic patterns in otherwise "clean" winds. To overcome these effects, they considered locating the turbines further from the building and closer to the water, but they were concerned about the site impacts and loss of educational opportunities if they were to do this. In the end, they decided to mount the two turbines on seventy-foot poles to mitigate the issue. The turbines, which effectively bookend the Brock Environmental Center, make a dramatic statement upon approach, and the sound of the spinning blades adds to the sensory experience of the site.

"The renewables would have been almost invisible without the turbines," says Lappano.

"The environmental community has been conflicted about wind power. On the one hand, there have been concerns about bird and bat mortalities associated with the spinning wind turbine blades. On the other hand, the consequences of rising greenhouse gas concentrations in the atmosphere due to the burning of fossil fuels are likely to be catastrophic.

While they could have met their net zero energy goal with photovoltaics alone, CBF took the courageous position of illustrating their support for wind power in their own facility. This was not without push back, but in the end, CBF has so much unquestionable credibility that their support promises to change the nature of the discussion in the mid-Atlantic region where they have great prominence. They didn't have to take this step, but bravely did so. This is significant leadership!"

RUSSELL PERRY
SmithGroupJJR

99

THE BROCK CENTER'S SOLAR ARRAY

Solar energy options had expanded since the Merrill Center was designed and built. One of the options the design team considered for the Brock Center was solar cells that were integrated into roofing materials. But the output of building-integrated photovoltaics (BIPV) was much lower than conventional PV modules, and the design team preferred an approach that allows for disassembly and facilitates replacement of modules. The team decided to mount conventional PV modules directly on the sloping portion of the Galvalume roof. This design feature would optimize the roof area and eliminate problems with modules being shaded by other modules.

To save space on the roof and to accommodate a future expansion of the PV array, the design team originally chose a module with 19 percent efficiency; however, they eventually realized that using a less efficient module would cut costs significantly, even as it increased the number of modules required.

The original array installed consisted of one hundred and forty-four 270-watt SunModule modules from American manufacturer SolarWorld and a centralized Fronius inverter system that included the capacity for additional modules. During the first three months of the audit year, the wind turbines were not performing as well as was predicted. Rather than risk not meeting the net zero energy goal, CBF decided to purchase twenty-four additional modules, bringing the total capacity of the array to 45.36 kW. The panels were fairly inexpensive and could be integrated into the existing inverter.

Both the wind turbines and the PV modules are tied into the building's main electric distribution panel. Any excess energy is fed into the electricity grid. A building automation system tracks both energy production and consumption; CBF provides a dashboard so that visitors and staff can view data in real time. **cbf.org/brockdashboard**

Photo: Skyshots Photography

THE HEALTH PETAL

Connecting with Nature

Photo: Prakash Patel

103

SUMMARY OF THE LIVING BUILDING CHALLENGE VERSION 2.1 HEALTH PETAL

Petal Intent

The intent of the Health Petal is to focus on the major conditions that must be present to create robust, healthy spaces, rather than to address all of the potential ways that an interior environment could be compromised. Most buildings provide substandard conditions for health and productivity. There is a direct correlation between decreased comfort and increased environmental impacts, since solutions in the physical environment to improve well-being are often energy-intensive and wasteful.

Petal Imperatives

- Civilized Environment
- Healthy Air
- Biophilia

104

The open office environment at the Brock Center ensures everyone enjoys access to natural light and fresh air.
Photo: Dave Chance

"So many studies show the benefits of natural light. As an administrator, I saw that in my staff [when they moved from their previous offices to the Merrill Center]. Attitudes shifted; it was an amazing transition to watch. After the move, if something went wrong, people fixed it themselves and were less likely to complain about it than before. At the Brock Center, we're seeing the same emotional reaction to daylight."

MARY TOD WINCHESTER
Chesapeake Bay Foundation

Restoring and maintaining the connection between people and nature, to the benefit of both, is one of the Chesapeake Bay Foundation's primary strategies for saving the Bay. Promoting the biophilic, human-nature connection was also a design priority for the Brock Environmental Center, as reflected in the building's siting, orientation, and form.

The Brock Center offers an appealing vision of the modern workplace. There is an abundance of fresh air and natural light. Every space, from the lobby to the office area to the cozy staff kitchen, includes views of water, marsh, and sky. The many windows and doors blur the lines between the inside and the outside, and sheltered outdoor spaces around the building invite visitors to step outside and connect with the site. The building even smells good.

The intent of the Health Petal is to focus on the major conditions that must be present to create robust, healthy spaces. One of these conditions, as outlined by the Standard's eighth Imperative, is that every occupiable space include operable windows. At the Brock Center, no desk is located more than twelve feet away from an operable window, ensuring that every staff member enjoys fresh air and views of the shoreline. Individual workstations are smaller, in part to make room for shared collaboration spaces.

The team imported the concept of the open office from the Merrill Center. Mary Tod Winchester recalls that some staff were initially resistant to the open plan at Merrill, but once staff understood the consequences of individual office spaces—a significantly larger building, and unequal access to daylight and natural ventilation—they adjusted to the more flexible arrangement. Staff who moved into the Brock Center from the Norfolk office also had to give up private offices; however, they gained much more.

105

The Health Petal: CONNECTING WITH NATURE

"With the open design, we've been able to get more people in the same space. We've been able to expand and contract—it's flexible. Staff were a little hesitant about the open design at first, but we worked with them and educated them. All we had to do was say, we'll give you your own individual office, but we're going to have to build a much bigger building for the same number of people. And you saw the light bulb go off, and they said, 'well, we do have to practice what we preach.'"

MARY TOD WINCHESTER
Chesapeake Bay Foundation

"Decades ago, we understood the relationship between food and health—"you are what you eat." Society is increasingly understanding the relationship between the places we inhabit and our health—"you are where you dwell." Concepts like daylighting, natural ventilation, healthy materials, and access to nature not only conserve resources; they also enhance our well-being."

GREG MELLA
SmithGroupJJR

HEALTHY AIR, HAPPY EMPLOYEES

The Living Building Challenge Standard protects the health of occupants, manufacturers, suppliers, and the environment by prohibiting Red List materials from being used in and around the building. CBF also took voluntary measures that are supportive of health. For example, the building does not include any carpeting, which can harbor dust, allergens, and other harmful substances within its fibers.

Imperative 09: Healthy Air sets forth requirements for specific measures that impact indoor air quality. These demands include internal and external dirt track-in systems, separate ventilation for kitchens, bathrooms, copy rooms, janitorial closets, and chemical storage spaces, and a prohibition on smoking. This Imperative also requires that carbon dioxide, temperature, and humidity be monitored, and that ventilation rates comply with ASHRAE 62. Finally, it requires testing for total volatile organic compounds (TVOCs) and respirable suspended particulates both prior to occupancy and nine months after occupancy has begun.

Ventilation is critical in low-energy buildings, which are usually exceptionally well-insulated and airtight. Although the windows

at the Brock Center stay open as much as possible, mechanical ventilation is necessary when they are closed. The building relies on a single 1,400 CFM dedicated outside air system, or DOAS, which supplies outside air directly to each occupied space, at rates specified by ASHRAE 62.1. The unit heats, cools and dehumidifies the outside air; supply ducts are fitted with filters with a MERV 13 rating, which remove at least 90 percent of dust particulates.

All high-occupancy spaces within the building, such as the conference room, contain sensors that monitor CO_2 levels and trigger the DOAS unit to deliver more outside air to the space, keeping concentrations of indoor air contaminants low. In addition to the DOAS unit, the janitorial closet and catering

Track-in grilles were installed strategically, ensuring that any person approaching from any location will pass over ten feet of steel grille before entering the building.

▶ **POINT OF ENTRY**
　 EXTERIOR FOOT GRILLE
　 INTERIOR FOOT GRILLE
　 INTERIOR CONDITIONED SPACE
　 ELEVATED DECK

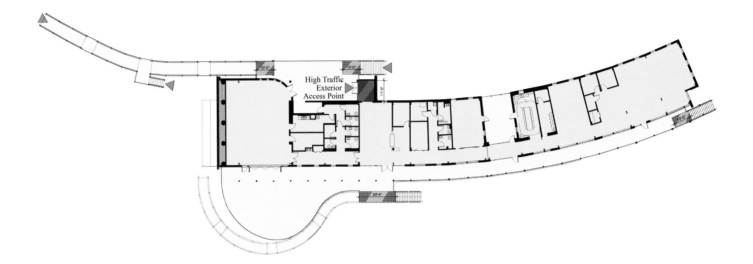

kitchen are each vented separately using ceiling-mounted exhaust fans. The composting toilets ventilate the bathrooms by pulling air into the toilets and down to the composting unit, which is itself exhausted to the outside. This ventilation strategy creates negative pressures in the bathrooms, which helps prevent odors, and a battery back-up ensures the bathrooms will remain odor free even during power outages. There is no enclosed copy room; instead, the copier is located in an open work room. The machine is not used enough to warrant venting as per LEED v4.

Sensors located outside the building measure the outside air temperature and humidity levels. Mechanical engineer Brian Coffield established temperature and humidity ranges where the outside air could be used to meet building loads (between 45 and 78 degrees F and below 88 grains per pound absolute humidity, respectively). If exterior conditions fall outside of this range, the building management system switches both the DOAS and the VRF systems on to provide outside air and space conditioning. If the exterior conditions fall within the acceptable range, the

BMS switches the mechanical systems off and notifies building occupants (via text, email, and a green light mounted inside the building) that it is time to open windows.

Because CBF's field programs bring many children in and out of its doors, an effective system for keeping the field debris outside was essential. The building's design funnels nearly all visitors and staff to a single entry, where they must cross over a stainless steel foot grille before entering. In addition, foot grilles are located at the top of each ramp and set of stairs leading to the elevated decks.

107

The comfortable staff kitchen and
light-filled hallway give employees
and visitors opportunities to interact.
Photo: Dave Chance

LIVING WITH A LIVING BUILDING

Although designers and builders can control the materials used in the construction of buildings and ensure systems for adequate cycling of fresh air are in place, occupant behavior—how the building is cleaned and maintained, what products are allowed, and how windows are used—greatly impact indoor air quality once the building is commissioned.

Red List vetting has continued since the Brock Center opened. Building Manager Chris Gorri researches cleaning products to ensure they are free of toxins; no chlorine-based products are allowed. Personnel clean the building early in the morning, before regular staff hours, using non-toxic products that do not create lingering odors. And the windows are open as much as possible.

CBF knew from experience at the Merrill Center that their staff are prone to favoring natural ventilation, even on days when temperatures fall above or below the "comfort band." Chuck Foster, Chief of Staff at the Merrill Center, expected passive heating and cooling (open windows) to be used about 10 percent of the time. CBF conducted a study and found that natural ventilation is actually used 34 percent of the time. Rich Moore, the Merrill Center's Building Manager, has noticed that on "open window days," people tolerate a much wider range of temperatures before they start to complain of being too hot or too cold. Chris Gorri has observed the same trend at the Brock Center.

Although it may be difficult to quantify, the building is positively impacting employees,

says Gorri. "Every now and then a staff member will stop me and say, 'I feel so energized when I'm here!'" One visiting staff member who is prone to migraines never developed a headache after spending a day at the Brock Center despite having forgotten to take her migraine medication. A visiting consultant who conducts educational training noted that, after holding a session at the Brock Center, her trainees did not experience the energy lull that typically strikes after lunch. The combination of healthy air, natural light, fresh air, and pleasant views no doubt fosters health and well-being. But there may be another factor at play as well.

The scale and layout of the Brock Center ensures that people will have spontaneous, face-to-face interactions. In any given day, children file through the building on the way to field programs. Tour groups and random visitors pass through the lobby and onto the deck. People linger in the light-filled hallway, talking. The Brock Center shows that robust, healthy spaces promote connections not only between humans and the outdoors, but with each other.

> *"The biggest compliment that we get about the building is that it feels so comfortable. Whether that's because of the choice of paints or the curves, nothing feels sterile or like a 'normal' office building. Every aspect of the building has a bit of fun in it."*
>
> **CHRIS GORRI**
> Chesapeake Bay Foundation

Photo: Dave Chance

DESIGNING WITH NATURE

The Living Building Challenge Standard mandates the incorporation of biophilic elements into the design of buildings in order to nurture the innate human attraction to natural systems and processes. The ILFI considers this natural connection essential to physical health and mental well-being. Much like the human tropism toward beauty, this intuitively felt truth has been ignored too often in modern architecture.

Recognition of biophilia, or the inherent human affinity for our natural world, was a part of the Brock Center design from the earliest sketches right up to the time when the final coats of paint were applied. For guidance, the design team paid heed to Dr. Stephen R. Kellert's Six Principles of Biophilic Design. Although it is easy to experience the elegant natural design elements of the Brock Center and intuit that it is informed by the philosophy of biophilia, it is also possible to identify specific features by Kellert's biophilic design categories:

ENVIRONMENTAL FEATURES: Elements include the use of color and natural materials, and the incorporation and enhancement of views and vistas. Before choosing colors for the building, the design team studied photographs of the site during different seasons. The Brock Center's palette complements and mimics these natural color schemes, which include the blues

Photo: Dave Chance

of The Chesapeake Bay, the green of Loblolly Pine needles, the straw blond of salt meadow plants, and the rusty orange of resident marsh grasses. Many of the building's features work together to enhance views and encourage visitors to connect with the landscape. These features include the building's long form, abundant windows, elevated grade and its orientation on the site.

NATURAL SHAPES AND FORMS: The Brock Center incorporates natural shapes and forms inside and outside the building, and on the macro and micro scales. The entire building was designed to resemble an animal; in particular, the conference room, with its curved roof, hints at the terrapin's shell, a gull's wings, and an oyster's shell; the overlapping zinc shingles resemble fish scales. The interior vaulted space curves, and the beams recall the curving limbs of live oaks that grow on the site.

NATURAL PATTERNS AND PROCESSES: This category includes natural patterns on different scales, called fractals, and elements that suggest the passage of time, among others. In the Brock Center, the inward-spiraling pattern in the conference room flooring creates a central focal point and makes a complicated room cohesive. Similarly, the diagonal flooring pattern in the lobby and open office areas help integrate the different parts of the building into a unified whole.

LIGHT AND SPACE: The many windows, abundant natural light and high ceilings in the office area and conference room create feelings of spaciousness and evoke a natural environment. In contrast, the lower ceilings of the corridor, combined with the continuous curve, direct attention out the windows. The dog trot—essentially an outdoor room within the building mass—serves as a transition space between indoors and outdoors.

111

HOW IS THE BROCK CENTER LIKE AN OYSTER?

The design team admired the native oyster not just for its pleasing physical form, but for its functions, which are so vital for the health and water quality of The Chesapeake Bay, and which matched many of the goals for how the Brock Center would function. This approach marries biophilia with biomimicry—the practice of taking cues from natural forms and processes to create better buildings, materials, and products that are nontoxic, low energy and do not produce waste.

Here are some of the characteristics of oysters that the design team looked to for inspiration:

- Oysters are tolerant organisms, able to withstand wide variations in temperature.

- Oysters provide valuable shelter and habitat for many other estuarine organisms.

- Oysters filter the water and remove sediment, improving water quality.

- Oysters stabilize the bottom and buffer the shoreline from erosion.

- Oysters transform trash into treasure by encapsulating irritants and turning them into pearls.

- Oysters open and close for protection, responding to environmental conditions.

112

"Now that we've been in the building awhile, we're starting to appreciate different things. For example, the feel of the building changes with every season, as it reflects something different from the natural landscape outside. But it always smells the same. From the very beginning, Brock never smelled like a construction project—it just smelled natural."

CHRIS GORRI
Chesapeake Bay Foundation

PLACE-BASED RELATIONSHIPS: The siting and form of the Brock Center pays close attention to the site. The building's horizontality reflects the topography, with its low-growing marsh grasses and uninterrupted views of the water and sky, and its gentle curve mimics the shoreline. The Brock Center also pays homage to historic and indigenous structures, including longhouses, which are characterized by their long form, vaulted space, and overall simplicity. The Brock Center also draws from the plantation houses of European settlers, notable for their elevated structure and wrapping porches, and from Southern dog-trot houses, which utilize a central breezeway to unite public and private spaces.

EVOLVED HUMAN-NATURE RELATIONSHIPS: This final category includes concepts such as prospect and refuge; exploration and discovery; and affection and attachment. The Brock Center addresses many of these functions simultaneously. The physical approach to the Center decouples humans from their cars; the peaceful, forested environment creates a literal physical transition from the fast-paced, car-centric built environment to a slower-paced, more sensual place. The education pavilion serves as a place of prospect and refuge—its roof protects people from the elements but does not cut them off from the smells of the marsh and sounds of the rain. The pavilion also serves as a classroom for CBF's educational programs—a place that nurtures exploration and discovery.

113

THE
MATERIALS
PETAL

Honesty and Transparency

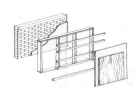

The Materials Petal: **HONESTY AND TRANSPARENCY**

SUMMARY OF THE LIVING BUILDING CHALLENGE VERSION 2.1 MATERIALS PETAL

Petal Intent

The intent of the Materials Petal is to induce a successful materials economy that is non-toxic, transparent, and socially equitable. Throughout their lifecycle, materials are responsible for many adverse environmental issues including illness, squandered embodied energy, pollution, and resource depletion. The Imperatives in this section aim to remove the worst known offending materials and practices. When impacts can be reduced but not eliminated, there is an obligation not only to offset the damaging consequences associated with the construction process, but also to strive for corrections in the industry. At the present time it is impossible to gauge the true environmental impact and toxicity of the built environment due to a lack of product-level information.

Petal Imperatives

- Red List
- Embodied Carbon Footprint
- Responsible Industry
- Appropriate Sourcing
- Conservation and Reuse

CHESAPEAKE BAY FOUNDATION
BROCK ENVIRONMENTAL CENTER

The Brock Center incorporates simple, naturally beautiful materials such as zinc and wood. Photo: Dave Chance

The Brock Environmental Center is a naturally beautiful building, and most people are struck by the honesty of the materials it incorporates: the wood cypress cladding; the zinc and galvalume roofing; the extensive use of wood inside the building. SmithGroupJJR's overarching strategy was to demonstrate a preference toward minimally-processed, bio-based materials over heavily-processed, complex synthetic and chemical-based materials. Not only did this make the materials vetting process easier, the approach dovetailed with the project's biophilic design goals, and the concept that people generally prefer natural materials to synthetic ones.

Greg Mella describes SmithGroupJJR's approach simply: Use "caveman" materials such as stone, wood, and metal; limit the palette in general; and utilize as many salvaged materials and products as possible. This strategy for material selection was deeply influenced by the experience of creating the Merrill Center. SmithGroupJJR identified several key lessons learned from that project, the first of which was to involve the contractor early on. Normally, the architect specifies materials and the contractor procures materials. A Living Building Challenge project requires much closer coordination to meet the Materials Petal requirements. Hourigan Construction, with its comprehensive approach to construction management, was an ideal partner. This close architect-contractor

117

When selecting materials, the Brock Center team considered many aspects of sustainability, including the energy required to transport the materials to the site.

"Our material selection approach can be likened to shopping in a supermarket, where you fill your cart with items from the perimeter aisles of the store—produce, meat, fish, bread— and avoid the heavily processed alternatives found in the center aisles. At the Brock Center, we favored the "Cuties" and Clementines in lieu of the Cap'n Crunch."

GREG MELLA
SmithGroupJJR

collaboration helped keep the project on schedule, within budget, and ensured it would successfully meet the Living Building Challenge criteria.

Mella likes to say that the greenest material is the one that is not used. With the Merrill Center, SmithGroupJJR pushed this concept by specifying materials that could be left unfinished, and materials that could perform more than one function. For instance, the undersides of the structural insulated panels (SIPs) for the roof were left exposed, yet served well as the finished ceiling.

With the Brock Center, there was one significant change in the approach to materials, which reflects the evolution of the industry's thinking around sustainable building. Many of the materials used in the Merrill Center, such as bamboo, cork, and engineered wood, were soon seen in green buildings all over the country.

These choices emphasized recycled content and rapidly renewable resources. Today, the approach has become more sophisticated, stressing multiple rather than single attributes, considering such things as embodied energy, transportation energy, longevity, contribution to indoor air quality, and how the material functions in the building.

The selection of the roofing at the Brock Environmental Center reflects this more holistic approach. The roof material needed to meet the Challenge's Red List and Appropriate Sourcing Imperatives, but it also needed to be suitable for rainwater collection in order to comply with the Water Petal, and support photovoltaic panels to promote the Energy Petal. Finally, the roof needed to be visually appealing and conform to the curved design in support of the Beauty Petal and the Biophilia Imperative.

THE A TEAM

Chris Brandt had been astute when he identified the need to hire a full-time Quality Control Manager to handle the Materials Petal requirements. That person was Tyler Park, a young graduate of Virginia Tech, who was hired during Schematic Design.

Greg Mella brought architect Dafeng Cai on to handle the materials from the architect's side. The two men worked closely with Janet Harrison and later, with Megan O'Connell of Skanska USA. Cai was the point person for all of the materials documentation; Harrison served as mediator between Cai and Park and sought clarifications and answers from the ILFI Dialogue, when necessary.

This close collaboration between architect and construction manager was unusual, but necessary. The core team of Cai, Park, and Harrison divided the materials among themselves, according to CSI MasterFormat division, and began holding weekly conference calls to provide updates and discuss specific problems. Park had the help of several interns during the years-long process. Katie Cuellar and Project Administrator Janice Robbins helped with documentation; Sustainability

Analyst Sydney Covey joined the team after construction. The weekly calls often included Cuellar, Covey and Robbins of Hourigan Construction, Greg Mella of SmithGroupJJR, and Paul Willey—and later, Chris Gorri—of CBF.

Hourigan's many subcontractors also played a critical role in tracking materials. Plumbing and electrical contractors, carpenters, roofing contractors, and HVAC contractors were each responsible for the products and materials associated with their aspect of the job, and were required to obtain product documentation and submit letters.

"We put a lot of ownership on them to deal with their suppliers and manufacturers," says Park. Some willingly took on the task; others refused or neglected to send the letters. In these cases, Park or someone else from the vetting team had to take on that task as well.

A STEEP LEARNING CURVE

Vetting the materials was a step-by-step and often tedious process. The first task was to determine whether the manufacturer would or could provide a public document that included a list of 100 percent of the product's ingredients. If they could not, they were pushed to provide this information.

At the time, the ILFI did not provide a template for a letter requesting information from manufacturers, so Cai, Park, and Harrison developed their own. However, once they had gotten deep into the process, they realized that their letter was not getting the job done.

As with the subs, some manufacturers were more cooperative than others. Many had never heard of the Living Building Challenge before and they did not understand what the team was trying to accomplish.

"We learned that some manufacturers were signing letters without really understanding them," says Cai.

They discovered that one letter could not accommodate all products and materials, which ranged from the simple—concrete, Galvalume roofing, and framing lumber, for example—to the complex—heat pumps, wind turbines, and ceilings fans, to name but a few. After much deliberation, they developed two letters: one for "simpler" materials; one for materials with complex components. Manufacturers were required to list all of the components for simple materials. But for complex products that included over ten components, manufacturers only had to provide information on the first eleven. Harrison, Cai, and Park decided that percentages were not as important as whether or not a product contained Red List ingredients, so the letter simply included spaces for the "top eleven" ingredients. It was up to the person filling those blanks to rank the ingredients by size. The manufacturer was also required to acknowledge that none of the non-listed ingredients contained Red List items.

Even after they refined the letters, the process was not perfect, and often the team had to follow up for more information. This further inquiry led to frustration on the part of manufacturers, who at times did not know the answers or felt they had already spent ample time and effort on their letters, only to have them rejected as not good enough or incomplete. A few manufacturers were unusually cooperative; Big Ass Solutions, for example, which provided the Haiku ceiling fans for the building, responded to multiple requests for more information with details about the composition, percentages and sources of sixteen material components.

"In the end, Big Ass Solutions became a proponent of the Living Building Challenge," says Harrison. "Now they have case studies for multiple LBC projects on their website."

Even the core team members did not always agree on how far to push the process. Cai was determined to stick to the letter of the Materials Petal requirements, and he often rejected submittals for lack of complete information. Park recalls one moment when, out of frustration, he created a sketch showing the breakdown of a wind turbine. The turbine was comprised of several elements, each of which could be broken down into several more. This meant vetting hundreds of materials—all for one product.

Often the team would come to a crossroads where they would have to decide whether to push a manufacturer for more information or whether to start over with another company. Ultimately, they had to decide case by case.

The Living Building Challenge guidelines did not provide specific answers. There was no Materials Petal handbook at the time. Instead, Harrison used the Dialogue to work through questions.

"Our definition and understanding of what was required evolved over time," says Cai.

Ultimately, the team's success in meeting the Materials Petal requirements came down to hundreds of unglamorous hours.

"It takes time," says Park. "A lot of phone calls; a lot of emails—there's really no way around it."

PRODUCT VETTING AND DOCUMENTATION PROCEDURES

This chart illustrates the complex process that was used to select and vet materials.

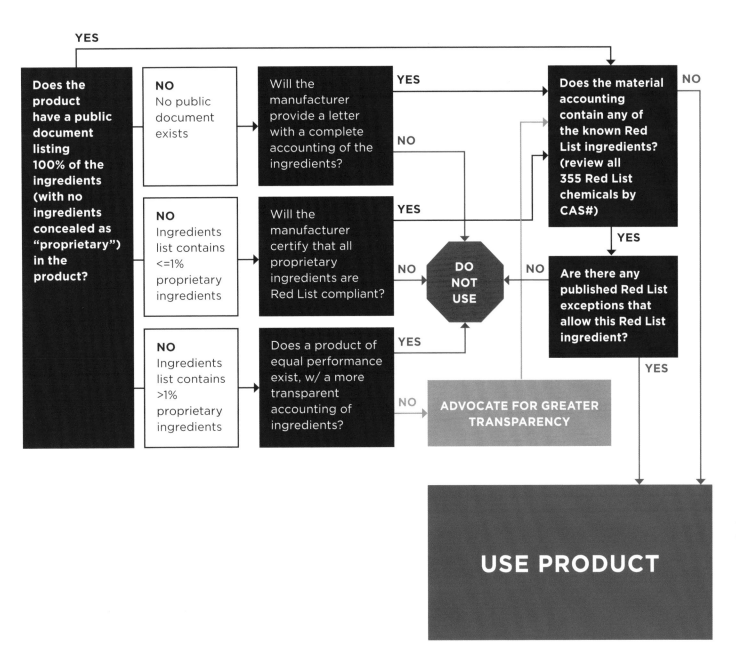

YES

Does the product have a public document listing 100% of the ingredients (with no ingredients concealed as "proprietary") in the product?

NO No public document exists

NO Ingredients list contains <=1% proprietary ingredients

NO Ingredients list contains >1% proprietary ingredients

Will the manufacturer provide a letter with a complete accounting of the ingredients? — YES / NO

Will the manufacturer certify that all proprietary ingredients are Red List compliant? — YES / NO

Does a product of equal performance exist, w/ a more transparent accounting of ingredients? — YES / NO

DO NOT USE

ADVOCATE FOR GREATER TRANSPARENCY

Does the material accounting contain any of the known Red List ingredients? (review all 355 Red List chemicals by CAS#) — NO / YES

Are there any published Red List exceptions that allow this Red List ingredient? — NO / YES

USE PRODUCT

121

PUSHING FOR TRANSPARENCY

When the team traveled to Seattle and Portland for the ILFI's Living Future unConference and met with other project teams, Mella and Perry were surprised and somewhat frustrated at how little information there was about the materials and products used in their projects. In general, other project teams were reluctant to share that information—not because they did not necessarily want others to have it, but because they were hesitant to share information that might be inaccurate or incomplete. At the time, there was no Materials Petal Handbook and there was no Declare database. The Brock Center team felt that they were mostly on their own.

SmithGroupJJR decided to be completely transparent about the vetting process and to share their materials research database through the company's website in December 2012, well before the project even broke ground. The complete database of nearly 1,000 materials can still be accessed there today.

As a member of the Board of Directors for the Health Product Declaration Collaborative, Perry has also been deeply involved in an industry-wide effort advocating for greater transparency. The Health Product Declaration, or HPD, is a reporting tool used by product companies and manufacturers of products that are used in the built environment. An HPD report contains information about a product's ingredients and associated health hazards. The HPD standard was designed to provide information in a standardized format, so that it could be used with certification programs and tools, such as Cradle To Cradle and Declare.

In 2013, Perry led an effort prompting forty architecture firms, including SmithGroupJJR, to write letters to manufacturers demanding greater transparency and encouraging them to develop HPDs. These letters, along with Declare and a new credit under LEED v4 for the Materials and Resources category, are creating transformative changes in the building products industry.

Because there was no central database for accessing HPDs, Perry and Mella set one up through SmithGroupJJR's website. Today, thousands of HPDs can be accessed through SmithGroupJJR's searchable HPD Library.

122

"We would get submittals and product documentation and submit to the architect, and often we had to go back to the manufacturer for more information. Most GCs don't want to take on this ownership. I had a vested interest in making sure that all the time I had invested was not wasted, and that it was done right."

TYLER PARK
Hourigan Construction

"The Declare database is populating, but there were few resources at the time. Sometimes it felt like we were in the middle of nowhere, especially being located in Virginia."

MEGAN O'CONNELL
Skanska USA

"SmithGroupJJR, and Rus in particular, showed generosity and fearless corporate leadership when they decided to share the information on the materials, because it was bigger than lawyers or code officials. They knew this is a new world, and it's something we need to solve by coming together and saying, how can we help each other?"

ELIZABETH HEIDER
Skanska USA

Stenciling letters onto pipes using non-toxic paint allowed the team to avoid lettering that was made of PVC, a Red List item. Photo: Chris Gorri

IMPERATIVE:
RED LIST

The Red List Imperative stipulates that no product or material used in the project may contain any of the fourteen substances on a worst-in-class "Red List." When the Red List is extrapolated to include the many variations of the fourteen primary substances, it comprises nearly 800 items. As with many Living Building Challenge project teams, meeting the requirements of this Imperative proved one of the most difficult challenges of the entire project.

At times, meeting this Imperative required finding substitutions for commonly-used building materials such as PVC pipe for plumbing and PVC-insulated wiring. For the plumbing, Hourigan used copper piping for the majority of plumbing inside the building, and HDPE (high-density polyethylene) piping for the heat pump ground loops. For wiring, they found a solution with a company that utilizes cross-linked polyethylene instead of PVC insulation.

The team also took advantage of some pre-established Red List exceptions. The Proprietary Ingredients Exception applied to manufacturers that refused to divulge all of the ingredients, claiming some were proprietary. Such manufacturers were asked to sign a letter stating that none of the proprietary ingredients contained any Red List items. In every instance, the design

team followed up with those manufacturers, advocating that they embrace materials transparency. The Small Electrical Components Exception and Small Mechanical Components Exception applied to small components within complex electrical and mechanical products made from more than ten constituent parts. These include backflow preventers and other plumbing parts, HVAC control system components, and occupancy sensors, to name but a few.

Sometimes the team came up with creative solutions to avoid the Red List. For example, the letters used to label piping in the mechanical room is typically made of PVC. Megan O'Connell proposed stencilling the letters onto the pipes instead, using a paint that had already been vetted.

123

PICKING BATTLES

No one expected drywall, also known as gypsum board or "gyp board," to give the materials vetting team any problems. But once they began researching the product, they discovered an interesting dilemma.

Not too long ago, all drywall was manufactured using natural, or mined gypsum. But about twenty-five years ago, manufacturers began taking advantage of a new resource: flue gas desulfurization, or "scrubbing," which removes sulfur dioxides from the combustion gases produced by coal-fired plants. This process creates synthetic gypsum as a byproduct. Using this synthetic gypsum in drywall products keeps a waste material out of the landfills and captures fossil fuel emissions, and it allows projects to qualify for LEED points for recycled content; indeed, the LEED program was a big driver in the adoption of this practice. Today, virtually all U.S. drywall manufacturing facilities are located next to coal-fired energy plants.

However, there is a catch: synthetic gypsum contains mercury. Naturally-occurring gypsum does too but not as much. EPA tests of several drywall products from the United States and China revealed that the product with the highest mercury by far was made using synthetic gypsum.

There is a Red List exception for Unintentional Trace Amounts of Red List substances, but the team was not sure if synthetic drywall products qualified for the exclusion. So they posed the question in the Dialogue, an online platform for Living Building Challenge teams hosted by the ILFI. The response was clear: the exception only applied to naturally-occurring mercury in wallboard.

The search was on for a drywall product made with mined gypsum. The team discussed the issue with several manufacturers, including United States Gypsum Company. This company had plants all over the country, but none of the ones east of the Mississippi used 100 percent natural gypsum in the manufacturing process. Eventually, the company agreed to run a special batch in its Jacksonville, Florida, plant, using 100 percent mined gypsum from Nova Scotia, Canada. Consequently, the product complied with both the Red List and the Appropriate Sourcing Imperatives.

"It really came down to picking your battles," says Park. "How much diligence was enough? Where do we stop? What are the areas where we can get some change? For us, drywall was one of those."

The Living Building Challenge requires teams to offset carbon released during project construction.
Photo: Tyler Park

IMPERATIVE:
EMBODIED CARBON FOOTPRINT

The Embodied Carbon Footprint Imperative states that the project must account for the total embodied carbon impact from its construction through a one-time carbon offset in the Institute's new Living Future Carbon Exchange or an approved carbon offset provider.

CBF purchased 1,234 metric tonnes of carbon offsets through Sterling Planet to support a Landfill Gas to Energy project in Dartmouth, Massachusetts. The Greater New Bedford Landfill Gas Utilization Project diverts landfill gas for use as fuel in four reciprocating internal combustion engine-generator sets that are specially designed for combustion of LFG. Landfill gas (mostly methane) is generated during the natural process of bacterial decomposition of organic material contained in municipal solid waste landfills. If released into the atmosphere, it is a powerful greenhouse gas. This project captures this waste product and puts it to use as an energy-producing fuel, taking the place of natural gas, fuel oil, or coal.

Bleachers from Salem Middle School were transformed into interior wood trim at the Brock Center.

SALVAGING STORIES

The Brock Environmental Center is rich with stories about materials that enjoyed another life somewhere else. These stories draw people in, sparking their curiosity and making them more receptive to learning about other aspects of the building.

Early on, SmithGroupJJR put out a call for the types and volumes of salvaged materials that they were seeking. Christy Everett disseminated the list to her contacts in the Hampton Roads community. Acquiring some of these materials early in the process allowed SmithGroupJJR to integrate them into the design.

However, using salvaged materials also required flexibility on the part of SmithGroupJJR and Hourigan Construction—to entertain unusual options, to act on the spur of the moment, and to store materials on-site for long periods of time.

Here are just a few of the stories behind the materials that give the Brock Environmental Center its unique personality:

FROM ONE EDUCATION CENTER TO ANOTHER

CBF and SmithGroupJJR knew they wanted to use local salvaged flooring, but they had to be willing to wait for an opportunity. Finally, Tyler Park received a call: a middle school in Norfolk was being demolished, and the maple flooring from the gym was available. Park grabbed a hammer and a crowbar and retrieved some samples, which he sent to Mella. After getting the thumbs-up, he mobilized a local carpentry crew. The rest of the flooring was a commercially available reclaimed product that had an earlier life as fence posts from a horse farm in rural Virginia. To make the transition between the two materials work, the gym flooring was refinished and stained a consistent color, and the carpenters installed it at a 45 angle to the wider-planked oak flooring. The gym flooring can be seen throughout the building except in the main corridor and in the Oyster conference room; these two areas utilize the fence post flooring.

126

Bleacher seats from Salem Middle School's gym were also salvaged and transformed into window and door trim. The carpenters were asked to lightly sand and stain the lumber; consequently, nicks and carvings, including students' initials, are still clearly visible, giving clues to the material's former life.

FOUR INCHES

Park was lucky to score interior doors from a facility owned by a local municipal agency that was to be razed. The doors were in pristine condition, and there were enough to fulfill the entire interior door package . Like so many of the project's salvaged materials, the doors sat in a shipping container for months. When it finally came time to install them, the carpenters discovered a problem: All of the doors measured 6'8"—the standard size for residential construction. The openings in the Brock Center were sized for standards commercial doors—a full four inches taller. Park briefly considered purchasing doors elsewhere, but ultimately everyone agreed to work with what they already had. The carpenter proposed laminating one-inch strips of poplar trim together and attaching the pieces to the tops of the doors to make up the difference. He could have created a seamless transition, but the team decided to highlight rather than hide the mistake. Today, the doors are a talking point.

ONE FROM THE COMMUNITY

Some materials came from unexpected sources. A community member who had been involved in the fight against the Indigo Dunes development learned about some live oak trees that were to be sacrificed for a development about a quarter mile from the Pleasure House Point site. He was able to salvage the trees, and arranged with Christy Everett and Paul Willey to deliver them to the site.

Tyler Park hired a mobile sawmill to process the wood, and he and Willey stacked it so it could dry. It was stored off-site for over two years. There was some question as to whether the lumber complied with the Responsible Industry Imperative. It was not harvested on-site, and it technically was not salvaged lumber, since it had not been used in another building or project. In the end, Coastal Creations transformed the lumber into a podium for the conference room, and educator and artist Inga Clough Falterman used some of the wood to create a mural depicting the flora and fauna of The Chesapeake Bay.

SALVAGED MATERIALS SAMPLER

Item	Source
Solid wood interior doors	Local office demolition
Wood flooring	Reclaimed fence posts
Wood flooring	Salvaged gym flooring from local school
Cabinet doors	Wood paneling reclaimed from local office demolition
Cabinet hardware	Champagne corks collected by community
Interior wood trim	Salvaged bleachers from local school
Granite countertops	Salvaged office credenza
Mirrors and toilet accessories	Local hospital remodel
Lockers	Local high school remodel
Ceramic tile	Overstock left over from Merrill Center construction
Exterior rainwater cistern	Salvaged pickle barrels
Cypress siding	Reclaimed "sinker" logs
Lavatories and mop sinks	Local hospital remodel
Reception desk millwork	Salvaged pickle barrel

127

IMPERATIVE:
RESPONSIBLE INDUSTRY

The Responsible Industry Imperative stipulates that all wood used in a project must either be fully certified by the Forest Stewardship Council (FSC), come from salvaged sources, or be harvested from the site itself.

Fully certified wood requires that every link along the supply chain must have FSC certification, even the truckers. But 100 percent certified wood could not be sourced on the East Coast at that time. To work around this issue, the team used as much salvaged wood as possible; however, they could not avoid using virgin wood for some elements, such as dimensional framing lumber.

The Living Building Challenge 2.1 Appropriate Sourcing Imperative required that project teams "prove" that a given material is not available within the specified zone, and that expanding the search beyond that zone is required.

"Showing that what was available to us within our zone was not usable was just as time consuming as finding something that would work," says Park. Through a careful documentation process, which involved contacting several vendors in each zone, the team was able to utilize zone jumping exceptions to satisfy both the Responsible Industry and Appropriate Sourcing requirements.

Park worked with a supplier based in Richmond, Virginia to not only source the lumber, but to coordinate its treatment for rot and moisture resistance. Dimensional lumber and decking were sent to a facility in Georgia, where it was treated with copper azole, which is the most environmentally responsible wood preservative treatment for dimensional lumber currently available.

The custom orders had to exceed a certain volume for the wood mills and treatment facilities to accept them. Because none of Hourigan's several subcontractors had an order that was large enough, Park bundled all of the orders into one, which was ultimately delivered as a single shipment. This meant that some of the material had to be stored and protected on-site for several months.

One of the lessons learned is that some lumber dimensions are more readily available as FSC-certified than others. Had SmithGroupJJR understood this, they could have favored those dimensions in the original design. As a consequence, they had to make some creative decisions after the fact. This included a redesign of wooden structural elements so the team could utilize FSC-certified members that were readily available.

128

Sinker Cypress siding upon delivery to the Brock Center site.
Photo: Courtesy Hourigan Construction

SINKER CYPRESS: A CASE STUDY IN RESPONSIBLE INDUSTRY

The team wanted to use wood cladding on the exterior of the Brock Center, but they knew that the material would have to be able to withstand the harsh coastal environment. Cypress was an ideal choice.

This tree contains cypressene, an oil that makes the wood naturally rot resistant. Cypress lumber could be sourced locally as salvaged "sinker" logs that have been recovered from rivers and mill ponds in the Southeast United States. These logs, some of which are nearly a thousand years old, were harvested one hundred years ago or more. Approximately ten percent of them were lost while being transported on rivers or while awaiting processing in swamps and mill ponds. While the outer bark of these trees has rotted away, the heartwood is perfectly preserved and is characterized by its strikingly beautiful grain. And since it takes many years for this compound to accumulate in trees, these older "sinker" logs are more rot resistant than today's commercially harvested cypress trees.

Mella sourced the cypress from Krantz Recovered Woods, based in Austin, Texas. But there was some question as to whether this material met the Responsible Industry criteria. The team used the Dialogue to clarify the issue, first proposing that it was not possible to certify such wood under the Forest Stewardship Council certification program. The ILFI countered that, while FSC certification might not be possible, the product should be certified by the Rainforest Alliance Underwater Salvaged Standard. This standard ensures that the wood is legally harvested, does not exploit indigenous communities, and does not negatively impact the environment.

Krantz Recovered Woods was not certified by the Rainforest Alliance Underwater Salvaged Standard, but the ILFI, recognizing that few companies currently participate in the program, granted an exception allowing the use of uncertified underwater

Recovered cypress logs yield naturally durable and rot resistant wood that can stand up to coastal environments.

salvaged wood in this case. In exchange, the team had to provide permitting and ownership documentation from Krantz Recovered Woods, along with a narrative regarding indigenous people's rights. The team also had to write an advocacy letter urging the company to seek certification under the Rainforest Alliance certification program.

"I try to pick caveman materials and natural, simple products. But even that approach is far more nuanced when you get into sourcing and embodied energy. I hadn't realized that there were any zinc products domestically manufactured. The Living Building Challenge forced me to research opportunities, and I uncovered a solution I previously did not know about."

GREG MELLA
SmithGroupJJR

SETTING PRIORITIES

As the team learned, there are implicit weightings that must be considered when vetting materials, which are not immediately evident. For instance, when given the choice between a material that contains Red List ingredients but falls within an acceptable Appropriate Sourcing zone and a material that does not contain Red List ingredients but is further away, the second, Red List-free option is preferred.

Windows were "the great debate" of the Brock Environmental Center project, according to Tyler Park. There were many factors to consider: energy performance, aesthetics, operability, environmental attributes and, since the project is located in a hurricane zone, wind and impact resistance. Ultimately, only two manufacturers could provide windows that met all of the criteria: American company Alpen High Performance Products and Intus, which has manufacturing facilities in Lithuania. Mella felt that the Intus product was better for performance and aesthetics, but the ILFI advised that it was more important to support the domestic company, so the team decided to go with the Alpen windows.

But an issue arose during the permitting phase of the project. Because the Brock Center is located in a hurricane zone, the windows had to be tested by a third party to ensure they met the standards of ASTM E1886 and E1996. While Alpen stated that they believed their products would pass the test, they would not guarantee it. Intus, on the other hand, backed their product with a guarantee. The team felt they could not take this risk, and so in the end specified the triple-paned windows from Intus.

Working with the Lithuanian-based company proved challenging. Intus was required to obtain a chain-of-custody certification from the Forest Stewardship Council for its manufacturing facility.

There was the language barrier, and overseas manufacturing made it difficult to inspect the fabrication and threatened the construction schedule. Once the windows arrived, the team worked with ASSA ABLOY and switched out the hardware, because they felt the original hardware would not hold up in the coastal conditions.

In the end, perseverance and patience won out, and the beautiful, high-performance and operable windows are one of the Brock Environmental Center's most visually-prominent assets. The story of this one product emphasizes the nuances of the decision-making process faced by each Living Building Challenge project team.

The zinc roofing shingles, on the other hand, represent a material for which a domestic source was ultimately preferred. These striking and durable shingles are one of the materials that give the Brock Center its distinctive aesthetic. The team first sourced this product from a company called Rheinzink.

"The name should have tipped me off," says Park. "It's manufactured in the United States, but the material is from Germany." As this lay beyond the acceptable source zone for roofing material, the team had to go back to the drawing board. After much research, they found a Tennessee-based company that manufacturers zinc shingles.

Finding windows that met energy performance and
impact resistance criteria, as well as the Appropriate Sourcing
and Responsible Industry Imperatives, proved challenging.
Photo: Scott Wertz

In addition to incorporating long-lasting, durable materials, the Brock Center is "designed for disassembly."
Photo: Courtesy SmithGroupJJR

132

IMPERATIVE:
CONSERVATION AND REUSE

The Brock Conservation Management Plan considered material efficiency in all phases of the project, from conception to construction, occupancy, and eventual deconstruction.

In the design phase, much thought was put into how to prolong the life of the building and facilitate deconstruction and reuse of materials. Uncoated, panelized materials such as zinc shingles, standing seam roofing, panelized PV modules, and fastener-attached assemblies, can be disassembled to be reused or easily recycled. The desire to minimize waste over the anticipated life of the Brock Center informed the project planning, design, and material selection. CBF's commitment to environmental stewardship also informs the Brock Center's day-to-day operations, which minimize waste through diligent recycling and composting efforts.

Hourigan was diligent about incorporating scrap to minimize waste during construction—for example, using dimensional lumber scrap for blocking, and incorporating waste concrete as crushed aggregate to support the entry road and fire lane. Park was in charge of the on-site recycling effort. Fortunately, a local company called RDS was able to take commingled construction debris and sort it off-site at their own facility. The company was even willing to find markets for difficult-to-recycle items, such as drywall scrap. Through these efforts, Hourigan was able to achieve an overall recycling rate of 95 percent.

Some waste materials required extra effort. Unlike LEED, the Living Building Challenge sets recycling thresholds for certain categories of materials in addition to an overall recycling rate.

One such category is carpet and insulation. The Brock Center does not include any carpeting, which meant the team had to achieve a 95 percent recycling rate for all insulation scrap. There is no market for recycled rigid foam, so the team began exploring multiple options. They found a West Coast company that uses recycled foam to make surfboards, and began talking with an East Coast company about doing something similar. Riffing off a chair made of recycled foam, Paul Willey built a prototype out of foam scraps. Harrison also brainstormed with a professor in Salisbury, Maryland, who posted the problem on various Internet boards.

"We got a zillion responses," says Harrison. "There were a lot of dead ends." One of the biggest leads was a grant program that provides funding to companies in North Carolina, enabling them to purchase machines that process foam so that it can be returned to the manufacturing stream. Though they did not end up utilizing this option, it gave the team more freedom when specifying the insulation, because they were not limited to manufacturers who would take back unused scrap product. In the end, Owens Corning agreed to accept scraps of its FOAMULAR product at its manufacturing facility in Tallmadge, Ohio, where it was reground and used in new insulation. The scrap needed to be clean and not contaminated with any other construction debris, so Park designated a separate storage container for the foam pieces.

133

THE EQUITY PETAL

Welcoming Place for All

EXIT›

Photo: Prakash Patel

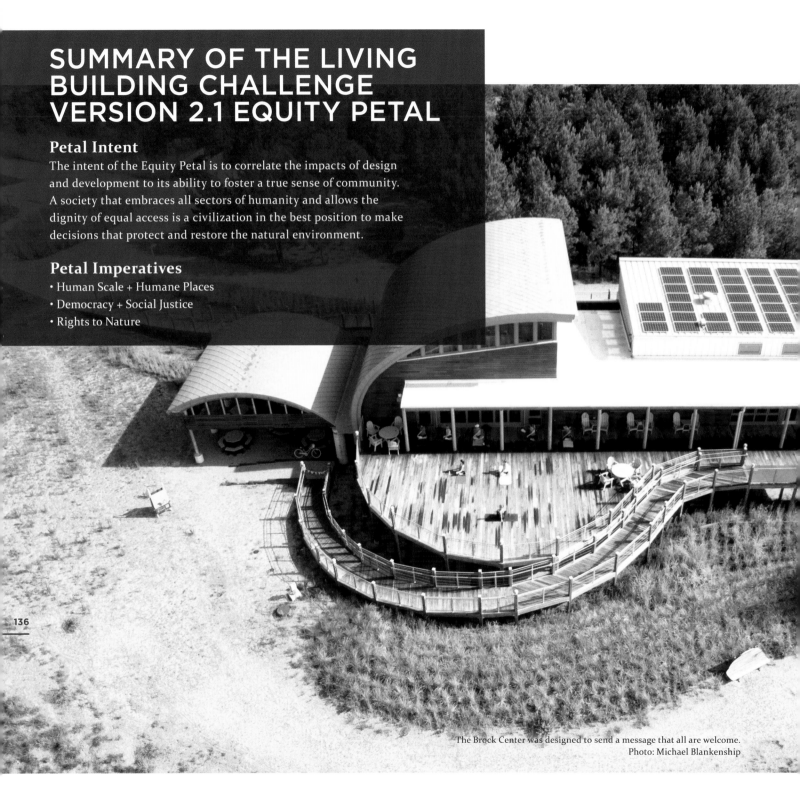

SUMMARY OF THE LIVING BUILDING CHALLENGE VERSION 2.1 EQUITY PETAL

Petal Intent

The intent of the Equity Petal is to correlate the impacts of design and development to its ability to foster a true sense of community. A society that embraces all sectors of humanity and allows the dignity of equal access is a civilization in the best position to make decisions that protect and restore the natural environment.

Petal Imperatives

- Human Scale + Humane Places
- Democracy + Social Justice
- Rights to Nature

The Brock Center was designed to send a message that all are welcome.
Photo: Michael Blankenship

"The intent of the Equity Petal is to correlate the impacts of design and development to its ability to foster a true sense of community. A society that embraces all sectors of humanity and allows the dignity of equal access is a civilization in the best position to make decisions that protect and restore the natural environment."

LIVING BUILDING CHALLENGE STANDARD 2.1

The Living Building Challenge recognizes that the built environment is a reflection of our collective attitudes toward social justice and equality. A society that holds the notion of private property sacrosanct inevitably produces inequalities: wealthy individuals and communities often restrict access to prime riverfront, beaches, and unspoiled natural areas, while poor communities often shoulder the burden of environmental degradation and pollution. The Equity Petal seeks to address these issues.

That Pleasure House Point was saved from private development and transformed into a city park is itself a victory in the spirit of Equity. Instead of restricting access to the shoreline to those residents of an exclusive condominium development, Pleasure House Point is open to all citizens, even as its ecological features and functions are protected.

"To me, one of the most interesting things about the Living Building Challenge is the emphasis on human scale—the whole notion that these places are about people, not cars. At the Brock Center, when you walk the forest path, you leave that car-centric world behind and literally pass through a gateway. I think that is such an important aspect, especially for a suburban project."

GREG MELLA
SmithGroupJJR

The forest path invites visitors to slow down.
Photo: Roberto Westbrook

138

IMPERATIVE:
HUMAN SCALE AND HUMANE PLACES

Imperative 16: Human Scale and Humane Places rests on the principle that the built environment should foster human-scaled rather than automobile-scaled places.

By design, the Brock Environmental Center sends a strong message of prioritizing people over cars by keeping most vehicles off the site altogether. This re-imagining of the role of the automobile is one of the project's great achievements. Keeping cars off the site not only ensures that the site's ecological functions are preserved, it shapes the experience of the site. The forest footpath and pervious paver walkway provide visitors and CBF staff with a very different experience from the one typical of a suburban development, with its wide streets, strip shopping developments, and asphalt parking lots. Visitors pass through a human-scaled gateway made from local driftwood. This literal portal provides a sense of arrival and serves as a threshold to a place where cars are no longer present; instead, this is a place for people—and for birds, wildlife, and native plants.

The Brock Center itself is human-scaled. Its one-story design ensures that the building does not dominate either the site or the people visiting it. The open office and single hallway ensure many opportunities for face-to-face interactions. Features such as porches and decks provide comfortable and inviting places for staff and visitors alike. Prominent outdoor spaces provide places for gathering, and the circular shape of the south deck promotes a sense of community.

CBF minimized signage, and interpretive signage was designed to complement the natural landscape and celebrate the creatures that live on Pleasure House Point. The City of Virginia Beach took a similar approach with very understated signage and unpaved footpaths that encourage people to experience the site as a natural area.

IMPERATIVE:
DEMOCRACY + SOCIAL JUSTICE

This seventeenth Imperative seeks to ensure that the project is equally accessible to all people, regardless of age, race, or economic status. Project teams are directed to use the Americans with Disabilities Act (ADA) and Architectural Barriers Act (ABA) Accessibility Guidelines to ensure access for persons with physical disabilities.

The Brock Environmental Center fulfills ADA requirements by providing three handicapped parking spaces right next to the building and near the entrance ramp. Everyone who enters the building's front doors walks or wheels up this same ramp. Not segregating individuals with disabilities from those people who are able to navigate stairs sends a message of equity and dignity. People can access the south side of the building by choosing from either a ramp or a set of stairs.

The building's single level and wide hallways ensure easy access for wheelchairs, and there are no thresholds that would create barriers for wheelchairs or those who have difficulty walking.

However, the goal was not simply to meet accessibility standards. "It's about effortless accessibility," says Greg Mella. "As designers, we try to go beyond the minimum requirements."

The Brock's bathrooms are a good example. None of the bathrooms include stalls, and they are slightly larger than ADA minimum requirements. As Mella himself learned, a few extra inches can make a meaningful difference for someone navigating a space in a wheelchair.

On August 8, 2014, just a few months before the building construction was completed, Mella suffered a serious bicycle accident. After surgery, he was confined to a wheelchair for four months. During this time he made a site visit to the Brock Center. There he experienced firsthand how the shift in perspective—from standing to sitting—significantly changes one's experience of the building.

All visitors utilize the same ramp when approaching the building's main entrance.
Photo: Dave Chance

139

"*The first time I went up the ramp in a wheelchair was eye-opening. How you interact with the building, how you experience the sightlines—it's all different. I can tell you firsthand that the few extra inches we provided in the bathrooms make these rooms considerably easier to use.*"

GREG MELLA
SmithGroupJJR

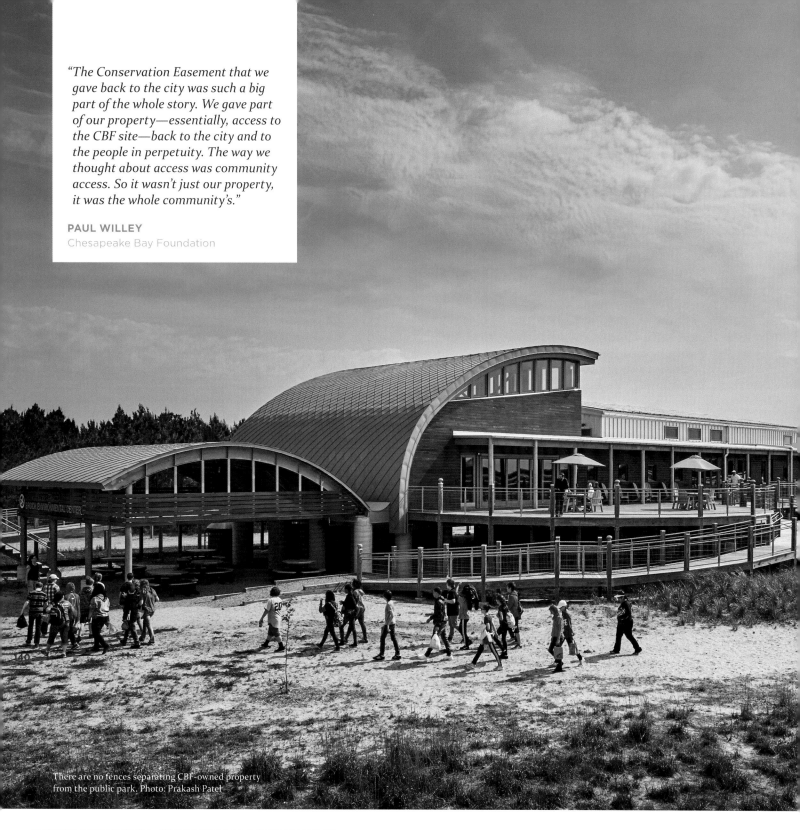

> *"The Conservation Easement that we gave back to the city was such a big part of the whole story. We gave part of our property—essentially, access to the CBF site—back to the city and to the people in perpetuity. The way we thought about access was community access. So it wasn't just our property, it was the whole community's."*
>
> **PAUL WILLEY**
> Chesapeake Bay Foundation

There are no fences separating CBF-owned property from the public park. Photo: Prakash Patel

"You can't see them, but there are plats and property lines and easements that define both CBF's property and the city park. We had to go back to the King James Charter to determine some of these lines. CBF gave the City a fifty-foot easement so the public can access the shoreline. But when you're standing out on the site, the experience is seamless."

BILLY ALMOND
WPL Site Design

IMPERATIVE:
RIGHTS TO NATURE

This Imperative states that a project may not block access to, or diminish the quality of, fresh air, sunlight and natural waterways for any member of society or adjacent developments.

CBF's educational programs bring many people through the building and onto the site. In addition, CBF shares the space with another environmental non-profit, Lynnhaven River Now, and offers meeting space free of charge to non-profits and local community organizations. But the Brock Environmental Center also sends a strong message that the site is open to the larger community.

The Center is uniquely positioned on a rare parcel of undeveloped shoreline within the City of Virginia Beach. People in the adjoining neighborhood had long considered Pleasure House Point a public resource, even when the property was privately held. It was important to both CBF and the City of Virginia Beach to preserve this continuity. To facilitate this goal, CBF gave the City of Virginia Beach a fifty-foot easement that runs along the shoreline. Today the property functions as a "dawn to dusk" park where anyone can still access the site during daylight hours for fishing, birdwatching, walking, or quiet contemplation. On any given day it is a common occurrence to see fishermen in waders standing in the marsh up to their waists fishing for trout while a school group files to the boat dock for a trip out to The Chesapeake Bay.

When people walk the shoreline trails, they are unaware when they have passed from city-owned property to CBF's land. The integration between the two properties is seamless; there are no fences and no gates, save for a small gate at the private boat dock that CBF uses for its educational field programs. Both CBF and the City of Virginia Beach sought to emphasize patterns that were already in place—walking paths, for example, largely follow paths that were already established.

The notion of being a good neighbor guided many design decisions. Although there was no requirement limiting the height of the building, it was kept to one story out of respect for the neighborhood to the north. The strategies for managing stormwater and greywater not only ensure that the building does not degrade water quality, but in addition, it has the potential for buffering the neighborhood from the impacts of flooding. And the Master Plan for Pleasure House Point will also improve water quality over the long term, as restored marshes fulfill their natural function as filters and buffers.

THE BEAUTY PETAL

Drawing from Place

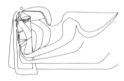

142

143

SUMMARY OF THE LIVING BUILDING CHALLENGE VERSION 2.1 BEAUTY PETAL

Petal Intent

The intent of the Beauty Petal is to recognize the need for beauty as a precursor to caring enough to preserve, conserve, and serve the greater good. As a society we are often surrounded by ugly and inhumane physical environments. If we do not care for our homes, streets, offices, and neighborhoods then why should we extend care outward to our farms, forests, and fields? When we accept billboards, parking lots, freeways, and strip malls as being aesthetically acceptable, in the same breath we accept clear-cuts, factory farms, and strip mines.

Petal Imperatives

• Beauty + Spirit
• Inspiration + Education

The Brock Center is a reflection of the shapes, colors and patterns of the surrounding landscape.
Photo: Prakash Patel

MARY TOD WINCHESTER
Chesapeake Bay Foundation

CBF and SmithGroupJJR approached the design of the Brock Center with the assumption that nature is synonymous with Beauty. They wanted the shapes, colors, and overall form of the building to reflect the plants and animals of The Chesapeake Bay, its topography, sinuous creeks and curving shorelines, and even the water itself. In this way, the concept of Beauty is so intertwined with the principles of Biophilia that it is impossible to talk about the one without mentioning the other.

The Beauty + Spirit Imperative invites project teams to include design features intended solely "for human delight" and which celebrate the culture and spirit of a particular place. When developing the initial design concepts for the Brock Center, the design team did not only consider energy efficiency, material use, and performance; they also wanted to create a space that welcomes and engages visitors and that honors the site and CBF's mission.

For inspiration, the team looked to the creatures and plants that inhabit Pleasure House Point: the oyster, with its strong, curving protective shell; the wind-swept live oaks with their twisting limbs; and the gull, with its gracefully arced and aerodynamic wings. The team also looked to the structures that define the region's human history: the longhouse, the kiva, the plantation house and dogtrot house. Drawing from all of these influences ensured that the building would be anchored in this very specific place.

Knowing that most visitors would be arriving from the northwest and on foot was an important factor driving the overall design. Two of the most striking and visible design features—the curving rooflines and the "head-and-tail" form—work in concert to draw people in.

145

When walking up the ramp, the first parts of the building visitors see are the outdoor education pavilion and an indoor conference space—the "head" of the Brock Center. Placing the education pavilion front and center was a deliberate choice to highlight CBF's educational mission and to provide opportunities for active learning upon arrival. The deeply curving roof of the conference room is clad with overlapping zinc shingles, which evoke fish scales and the shimmering silver water of The Chesapeake Bay. This dramatic arc is echoed by the gentler curve of the roof protecting the education pavilion.

The "tail" of the building trails off to the east, integrating with the marsh landscape. This section, which includes the lobby, offices, and smaller conference rooms, was kept low in profile to avoid blocking the views of the neighbors to the north, and kept narrow to facilitate ample natural ventilation and daylighting. The design team sought to avoid the aesthetics of a long narrow corridor by curving this portion of the building and lining it with windows. This way, a person walking the length of this section does not glimpse the end of the building until she or he has nearly arrived there; instead, the convex form draws the person's gaze outside. This vital connection with the outdoors encourages visitors to engage with the beauty outside the windows, and the curve evokes the very shoreline that is within view.

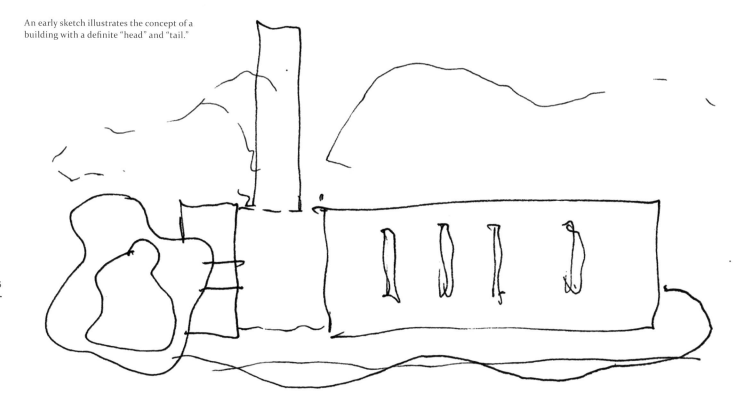

An early sketch illustrates the concept of a building with a definite "head" and "tail."

146

THE BEAUTY OF STORY

Inside and out, the Brock Center features shapes, textures, hues, and patterns which evoke the natural world. The building also incorporates many salvaged materials. Much as an older human face shows the map lines of a life's travels, these materials reveal stories about their past lives through scars, penetrations, and wear patterns.

For example, the window casing and trim was milled from bleachers from a nearby high school. Rather than sanding out the flaws, the carpenters lightly finished the wood, leaving intact the initials and graphics carved by students over the decades. The stories embedded within these materials add richness and a sense of continuity. For many visitors, these stories serve as a bridge, sparking their interest in other aspects of the building.

Local artists also contributed to the Brock Center with works inspired by The Chesapeake Bay and its inhabitants. Designers from Gropen, a Virginia-based design firm, created driftwood light fixtures in the lobby and the arched portal through which people walk on approaching the Center. Artist Inga Clough used thin slabs of live oak to create a mural for one of the conference rooms, painting depictions of The Chesapeake Bay wildlife on the organic canvases.

Features that speak to the community's involvement add another layer of richness to the Brock Center. These signs are both direct, as in the zinc tiles in the conference room and the donor plaque in the lobby, and implied. For example, cabinets and pulls and an artistic sign in the staff dining room are made from champagne corks collected by local neighbors and staff during the design and construction of the Brock Center. These corks hold the memories of celebrations and commemorate the contributions of the many people who have supported the project.

Photo: Chris Gorri

147

Photo: Dave Chance

"My biggest pet peeve is when people think that sustainability somehow limits you or compromises beauty. I think it's the opposite. Sustainable buildings are deeply connected to their site."

GREG MELLA, SmithGroupJJR

"When I was in architecture school in the late 1970s, there was some work on low-energy buildings, but they were the architectural equivalent of Birkenstock sandals. They were not beautiful or inspiring. Lower gas prices and the buildings being ugly conspired to set the movement back. It was impossible to make an economic argument, and you couldn't argue that the buildings were beautiful—they weren't. This is where the Living Building Challenge is so powerful: the Beauty Petal makes sure you pay attention to that as well."

ELIZABETH HEIDER, Skanska USA

"When people see the building and experience the property, and when they sit on the porch, they seem mesmerized— by the land, by the water, and by the building. It becomes an emotional connection. And then people start asking questions and it becomes an educational opportunity. That is really using Beauty to draw people in."

MARY TOD WINCHESTER, CBF

"When I made the pilgrimage to see the completed Brock Center and came around the corner and saw the building framed by the driftwood arch, I cried—I was overcome. The beauty of the building and the aspect from which you approach provides such an unrestricted view of the beauty of the inlet—such an appreciation of nature. The form embraces the place. I have not seen a better building—its scale and ability to function for CBF and to so elegantly express their mission."

ELIZABETH HEIDER, Skanska USA

Educating visitors about the Bay and sustainable building go hand in hand. Photo: Roberto Westbrook

COMPLEMENTARY MISSIONS

The other equally important dimension of the Beauty Petal is spelled out in the final Living Building Challenge Imperative: Inspiration + Education. The Imperative instructs project teams to provide educational materials about the operation and performance of the project to the public, and to open the doors to the public at least one day a year.

Public environmental education centers are uniquely positioned to educate many people; it's their raison d'etre. The Inspiration + Education Imperative is congruent with CBF's mission and a natural extension of the work they were already doing. From its inception, CBF has taken a holistic approach to education, one that includes an awareness of how its buildings and activities impact the very environment they are

trying to protect and restore. The organization takes seriously the call to practice what they preach, and have always used their buildings as teaching tools and inspiring examples of what can be. With the Merrill Center, CBF stretched far beyond educating the students and teachers enrolled in their programs. As the Merrill Center developed into a popular events venue, CBF staff found themselves in the position to educate a far

"People love stories, so we have devised many ways to work them into our tours. For example, people love the story of the bleacher wood, when we tell them it took two guys one hundred and twenty hours to scrape off all the bubble gum."

CHRISTOPHER GORRI
Chesapeake Bay Foundation

149

ENGAGING THE NEXT GENERATION

When Chris Brandt and his team were studying the Living Building Challenge in preparation for their interview with CBF, they discovered that Virginia Tech had built LUMENHAUS, a 500-square-foot net zero energy building that was completely powered by the sun. The project had earned first place at the International Solar Decathlon in 2010. In exchange for Virginia Tech's help with the presentation, Hourigan proposed creating a class that would enable Virginia Tech students to participate in the construction of the Brock Center.

Hourigan developed three-credit courses for twelve students. The first two semesters gave students hands-on experience with virtual construction. They participated in weekly M.E.P subcontractor and 3-D model coordination meetings and performed on-site quality control inspections using the mobile construction management software known as BIM 360 Field. The students immersed themselves into the details of the mechanical, electrical and plumbing systems and were tasked with leading a coordination meeting and identifying issues related to the mechanical loft spaces in the construction model. By pointing out conflicts with geothermal piping, photovoltaic inverter placement, and composter exhaust pumps, the subcontractors and students worked through crucial layout details related to a complex space. During the Fall 2013 semester, students helped monitor and analyze the Brock Center's net zero operating systems, as part of the Living Building Challenge certification process.

Other universities and industry companies, inspired by the collaboration between Hourigan and Virginia Tech, have expressed interest in initiating similar partnerships.

"We're still teaching virtual construction management and sustainability. That's what CBF is all about— educating kids so they can go out and change the world."

CHRIS BRANDT
Hourigan Construction

150

Chris Brandt instructs Virginia Tech students (above),
while Tyler Park (right) gives one of many presentations.
Photo: Courtesy Hourigan Construction

wider audience, one not necessarily interested in sustainability
or environmental preservation. And, as the Center quickly
earned status as a landmark green building, it began attracting
architects, builders, engineers, and business owners. Although
they embraced the opportunity to broaden their educational
reach, it was a trial by fire for CBF staff and for members of the
Merrill Center's design team. As they developed tour programs
and presentations to meet the growing demand, they grew into
their positions as ambassadors for the project.

CBF and SmithGroupJJR—and by extension, the rest of the Brock
team—took this lesson to heart. The team knew that the Brock
Center would be another high profile project and that many people
would want to learn from it. They took great care to document
every phase of the project in detail, and to be as transparent as
possible. This documentation included publishing the Materials
database before the project had even broken ground.

The education effort began early on with the Hampton Roads
community, the City of Virginia Beach, and employees of
various regulatory agencies. It took the form of public meetings,
presentations, and one-on-one conversations. Communicating the
holistic vision for the project required patience and perseverance.
Later, this experience was translated into one of the most
important lessons learned that CBF shares in presentations today.

People come to such presentations hungry for statistics on the
building's performance and the lessons learned. They are often

surprised when Mary Tod Winchester or another presenter
describes how CBF nurtured relationships with code officials,
and how important that was for successfully acquiring permits.

"Chris Gorri and I feel strongly that permitting agencies are
the most important group to reach," says Winchester. "The code
officials hold the keys to the door."

Many of the team members have shown great willingness to be
spokespersons for the project. Greg Mella, Mary Tod Wichester,
Tyler Park, Chris Gorri, and others have presented on various
aspects of the Brock Center at conferences around the country,
including the ILFI's annual Living Future conference, the Living
Product Challenge conference, and the USGBC's Greenbuild.
Chris Brandt and Tyler Park of Hourigan Construction gave close
to thirty presentations in just one year, presenting to industry
organizations such as the American Institute of Architects and
the Construction Management Association of America.

151

The Brock Environmental Center has been the subject of many articles and interviews for national industry magazines as well as more mainstream and local publications, from *Engineering News Record* and *Trim Tab* to *ARCHITECT* and *Fast Company* magazines. Hourigan Construction maintained an active blog throughout the project and during the audit year, adding construction updates, short posts on specific aspects of the Living Building Challenge, photographs, and videos, including footage taken from drone "flyovers" of the building in progress.

Equally important to the project's education mission, visitors to the Brock Center have the opportunity to learn about the building's design, construction, and operation firsthand. The Brock Center is open to the public year round. To date, over 50,000 people have come through the Brock Center's doors.

CBF worked with designers from Gropen to create interpretive signage in and around the building. CBF waited two years to install the majority of the signage, ensuring they had adequate feedback about the kinds of questions that visitors commonly asked. They knew it was especially important to have effective signage in place for those many times when CBF staff would not be on hand to answer questions about the building, the site, or the ecology and restoration of The Chesapeake Bay.

For those who like data, a digital dashboard in the lobby displays in real time the building's energy use, water use, and energy generated by the wind turbines and solar PV array (hour by hour, daily, or a different timescale choice). Anyone can also access the Dashboard in real time through CBF's website.

With help from Brock Environmental Center Coordinator Erica Nachman, Chris Gorri has created a regular tour schedule that includes about six tours per month: a standing tour every other Saturday, plus four during the week, including two evening tours. Gorri also organizes tours around special events.

CBF is fortunate to have a lively pool of volunteers. Fifty trained volunteers serve as tour guides, many of whom lead tours regularly and have developed distinctive styles. Here is where the stories do their good work, inviting young and old to smile, to ask questions, and to wonder what might be possible.

Photos (this page): Jay Fleming

152

OPPORTUNITIES FOR LEARNING

Environmental education programs at the Brock Environmental Center introduce thousands of students, teachers, and other groups to the unique flora and fauna of The Chesapeake Bay, and help them connect human activities to the estuary's health. CBF's courses combine many academic disciplines —earth science, biology, history, art, English and writing, mathematics, chemistry, civics, economics, government, and responsible citizenship. Participants conduct hands-on biological sampling, chemical analysis, and physical measurements, gaining a unique perspective on the relationship between water quality, fisheries, and economics.

The activities are many and varied. Students paddle up Pleasure House Creek. They pull seine nets along the beach and sample the marshes for macroinvertebrates. They inspect oyster beds. They collect native seeds in the salt meadow. They board the Jenny S, CBF's "floating classroom," where Captain Jimmy Sollner and Education Manager Yancey Powell introduce them to the Lynnhaven River and the greater Chesapeake Bay.

The Brock Center's education program has been so successful that a second program was launched in fall of 2016. Across the watershed, 40,000 students participate in CBF's education programs every year.

153

"I think that sharing [mistakes] makes for a more compelling story. You become more relatable. Nothing is perfect. I've had people come to me after a presentation and say, 'that was great—you told us what worked, but you also told us what didn't.'"

CHRISTOPHER GORRI
Chesapeake Bay Foundation

"When I get to the part about getting permits for the water—by going through that story—you see the audience go, wow, I never thought about that. We're teaching people how to think differently. Being able to tell these stories at a place like Greenbuild, where you have people who want to raise the bar by doing LBC projects, is a huge opportunity."

MARY TOD WINCHESTER
Chesapeake Bay Foundation

155

The Beauty Petal: **DRAWING FROM PLACE**

PART IV

Performance

Learning from the Brock Center

157

The "Unplugging Ceremony" marked the official opening of the Brock Center. (Left to Right) Jane P. Batten; Lieutenant Governor of Virginia Ralph Northam; First Lady of Virginia Dorothy McAuliffe; CBF President William C. Baker; Joan Brock; Harry T. Lester; Virginia Beach Mayor Will Sessoms. Photo: Roberto Westbrook

On November 14, 2014, the Brock Environmental Center officially opened.

There to celebrate the occasion were Chesapeake Bay Foundation staff, several members of the CBF Board and Task Force, major donors and community leaders, and many key project team members. The special day was marked with speeches from Virginia First Lady Dorothy McAuliffe, Lieutenant Governor Ralph Northam, philanthropist Joan Brock, and CBF President Will Baker. Baker also oversaw the "Unplugging Ceremony"—a symbolic disconnecting from the electricity grid in celebration of the project's net zero energy goal.

CBF hosted a grand opening celebration for the Hampton Roads community two days later. Thirteen hundred people attended the lively event, which included building tours, fish printing, boat trips, and seine net demonstrations. Visitors could also walk the nature trails and relax on the porch.

Over the years, many of the community members who had fought for the preservation of Pleasure House Point had become champions of CBF's new environmental center, even pitching in to prepare for the party being held in their honor. CBF had anticipated that their new building would draw attention; even so, interest has far exceeded expectations. During the first year alone, over 30,000 people visited the Brock Center.

"It's exactly what we want to happen," says Mary Tod Winchester. "When we build, we're raising the bar on green, but we also want to continue using the building as an education tool."

Meanwhile, CBF's Hampton Roads programs are going strong. The education program has been so successful that in fall of 2016, a second hands-on field program was launched.

159

Major storms tested the Brock Center in the fall of 2015 and 2016.
Photo: Chris Gorri

STORM-PROOF RESILIENCE

Of note, several significant weather events tested the Brock Center's resilience since it has opened, including major storms in the fall of 2015 and 2016. Hurricane Joaquin, a Category 4 storm that never made landfall, brought days of heavy rains and high winds in October 2015. A little over a year later, Hurricane Matthew wreaked havoc in Hampton Roads. Pleasure House Point flooded, and the water rose to knee-level under the raised building; however, the Brock Center and the wind turbines were unscathed, and all systems remained functional.

"We had a lot of pushback early in design and some of the community meetings were pretty tough, so it was really gratifying to have 1,300 of our best friends show up at the Grand Opening. What a difference between those initial meetings and the way the community has become family!"

MARY TOD WINCHESTER
Chesapeake Bay Foundation

THE PATH TO CERTIFICATION

The Brock Center began its year of performance monitoring in April of 2015. Janet Harrison was charged with gathering and submitting all relevant data and required narratives from various project team members. On April 28, 2016, CBF received the news that the Brock Environmental Center had been officially certified as a Living Building—the tenth project in the world to achieve full Living Building Challenge certification.

SITE

Imperative 01: LIMITS TO GROWTH

The Brock Environmental Center was built on a greyfield site that had not been developed with buildings, but which had been compromised by the dumping of dredge spoils, the introduction of non-native species, and other negative impacts. The Brock Center functions as an environmental education center, one of the acceptable uses in Transect L1. In addition, the project is contributing to the ongoing restoration of the site.

Imperative 02: URBAN AGRICULTURE

Because the Brock Center falls in Transect L1, this Imperative is not applicable.

Imperative 03: HABITAT EXCHANGE

CBF selected a project through the Living Future Habitat Exchange Program in order to fulfill this requirement. Through this project, CBF also contributed to the preservation of the 110 acres of Pleasure House Point, rare shoreline habitat in a densely populated region.

Imperative 04: CAR FREE LIVING

The Brock Center contributes to the creation of pedestrian-oriented communities by minimizing the presence of the automobile. By not providing parking on the site, the project sends a strong message of prioritizing people and the natural features of Pleasure House Point over the convenience of cars.

WATER

Imperative 05: NET ZERO WATER

The Brock Environmental Center collects, stores, treats and distributes all of its own potable water. The system includes rooftop rainwater harvesting, cisterns for storage, a comprehensive treatment train, pumps, and distribution plumbing. The system is plumbed with an optional connection to the City of Virginia Beach municipal water supply. Municipal water supplies the Brock Center's fire protection (sprinkler) system.

Imperative 06: ECOLOGICAL WATER FLOW

Rainwater flows from the Brock Center roof into cisterns located underneath the building. Any excess stormwater from the building roof is directed to rain gardens surrounding the building. Stormwater falling on the Winston Place parking area, on the walkway leading to the Brock Center, and on the ADA parking spaces next to the building infiltrates into the ground through the permeable pavers. During heavy rain events, any excess stormwater is captured in linear rain gardens that line the parking areas and walkway. Stormwater falling on the fire lane infiltrates through permeable gravel and into the ground. Greywater from the building is captured in a holding tank and pumped daily to a greywater infiltration dune next to the building. Wastewater is treated in five composting units; leachate from these units is captured and delivered to a nearby facility twice a year, where it is converted into struvite fertilizer.

161

Photo: Craig McClure

BROCK ENVIRONMENTAL CENTER FOR A LIVING CHESAPEAKE

RAINWATER SYSTEM: LESSONS LEARNED

Actual water use at the Brock Center is approximately 50 gallons per day, much lower than the predicted usage of 145 gallons per day. A lower water demand makes for a more resilient building. Less energy is required to pump and treat water. System components (filters, for example), will last longer, since they are processing less water per day. The cisterns and leachate tank can accommodate storage for a longer period, without changing in volume.

Water demand is greatly impacted by occupant behavior. At present, there is a shortage of benchmark data on how buildings use water. Collecting and sharing water use data will contribute to better databases.

The energy load associated with treating rainwater is lower than expected, in part because the building's water consumption is so much lower than was predicted. In addition, most of the energy required to treat rainwater is spent circulating ozone through the cisterns in order to keep the water clean and dissuade algae growth. The team assumed the ozone circulation pump would run eighteen hours each day, but as CBF discovered, much less pumping is required to keep the water clean, especially when the cisterns are not full and when temperatures are colder.

As was detailed in the Water Petal chapter, drinking the water revealed an issue with corrosivity, which was corrected with the addition of calcium carbonate. Everyone who samples the Brock Center's water agrees that rainwater tastes better than bottled water—a strong selling point for those who may have reservations about drinking rain.

Project teams should understand that pioneering water systems will inevitably require more time, extra expenses and requirements that may seem redundant. For instance, the Virginia Department of Health requires residual chlorine to be part of the treatment train. The State also requires an on-site state-certified waterworks operator and frequent turbidity monitoring. Finally, the system must be connected to the city's potable water system, which translates into additional materials and increased cost. As regulators become more comfortable with alternative systems, future project teams may not be saddled with the costs associated with having to provide these redundant municipal connections.

Teams should be prepared to start early and to build in extra time for the education and permitting process, and to find a champion to keep the process moving.

Treatment systems provide many teachable moments, and teams should be prepared to embrace these opportunities. With patience and persistence, oversight officials and contractors start to become believers, and in some cases, advocates.

WASTEWATER SYSTEMS: LESSONS LEARNED

As with the rainwater system, patience and persistence were required to educate permitting officials about both the greywater system and the composting toilet system. In this case, CBF's past experience—in particular with the Merrill Center, a 32,000-square-foot building that relies exclusively on composting toilets—went a long way to instilling confidence in permitting agencies.

As with the rainwater system, regulatory officials required "back-up" measures for both the leachate and greywater tanks. Both tanks include connections to the city sewer system, complexity which adds extra cost and materials.

The systems are working as well as expected. Signs in the bathrooms instruct users to add a pinch of sawdust in the toilet after each use. This simple action keeps the composters aerated, so the compost does not have to be turned as frequently. The leachate tank is emptied four times a year, and the leachate is sent to the Nansemond facility. Compost is raked several times a month. Once the system biologically establishes itself, finished compost will be harvested from each unit once a year.

ACTUAL ENERGY USE COMPARED TO ACTUAL ENERGY PRODUCTION

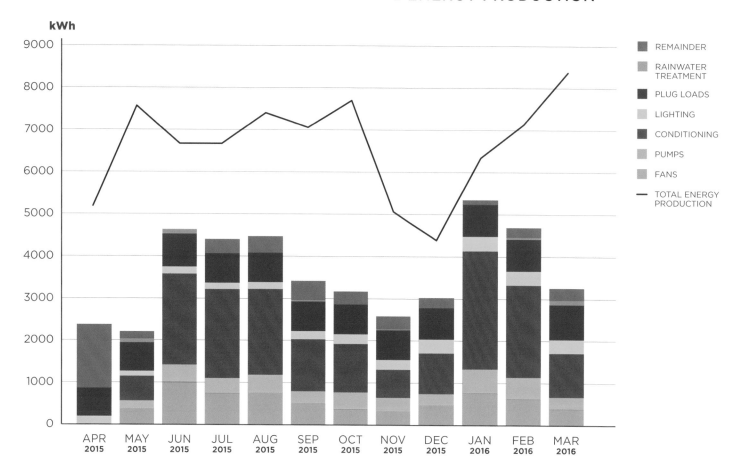

kWh

Legend:
- REMAINDER
- RAINWATER TREATMENT
- PLUG LOADS
- LIGHTING
- CONDITIONING
- PUMPS
- FANS
- TOTAL ENERGY PRODUCTION

Months: APR 2015, MAY 2015, JUN 2015, JUL 2015, AUG 2015, SEP 2015, OCT 2015, NOV 2015, DEC 2015, JAN 2016, FEB 2016, MAR 2016

ENERGY

Imperative 07: NET ZERO ENERGY

By the end of its audit year, the Brock Center's Energy Use Intensity (EUI) averaged 14.14, over 80 percent less than a typical building of the same size and nature. Especially impressive were the energy reductions in lighting and plug loads—loads which become more prominent in very energy-efficient buildings. Demands were reduced by 96 percent and 86 percent, respectively, when compared to the typical building.

The Brock Center was net positive every month during the performance year, and ultimately produced 1.83 times more energy than it consumed. The photovoltaic array produced 31.4 percent more energy than was predicted. In part, this was due to the fact that predictions were based on average production values for the modules over their service life. Since efficiency degrades over time, these values are lower than the modules' production immediately after installation. CBF also added twenty-four additional modules shortly after the audit year began, as the wind turbines were not performing as well as expected at that time, and CBF did not want to jeopardize its net zero goal.

Wind energy production is less predictable than solar energy, and although there were wide discrepancies between predicted and actual production from month to month, the Brock Center's wind turbines ultimately produced 99.6 percent of their targeted output during the performance year.

TRACKING WELLNESS

In spring of 2016, CBF and SmithGroupJJR partnered with the Catholic University of America to conduct a post-occupancy evaluation of the Brock Center. A team led by Hyojin Kim, assistant professor in the School of Architecture and Planning, performed an Indoor Environmental Quality (IEQ) assessment of the Brock Center based on the Performance Measurement Protocols (PMP) for Commercial Buildings that were developed by ASHRAE, CIBSE and USGBC. The PMP provides standardized methods for measuring and comparing the performance of occupied buildings for six areas: energy use, water use, thermal comfort, indoor air quality, lighting, and acoustics.

The evaluation included both subjective and objective components. First, staff were given questionnaires in which they were asked to evaluate how various EIQ factors—lighting, thermal comfort, indoor air quality, and acoustics—affected their productivity. Meanwhile, the objective assessment was performed with the help of an "IEQ cart," which included instruments that monitored air temperature, air speed, relative humidity, carbon dioxide, total VOCs, illuminance, and sound pressure.

Survey participants reported satisfaction levels that were above benchmarks in all but one category: acoustics. These results are significant, especially considering that the building utilizes mostly natural daylighting and relies extensively on natural ventilation. The main issue reported with acoustics was people talking nearby.

Kim believes that one of the factors contributing to such high satisfaction in the areas of thermal comfort, lighting, and indoor air quality is related to "adaptive opportunity." Staff at the Brock Center enjoy a high degree of control over the indoor environment; for example, they can open and close windows, operate ceiling fans, and open and close blinds. According to Kim, previous studies have reported significant and positive impacts on both improving comfort and reducing energy consumption by allowing people greater control over their own indoor environment and opportunities to adapt to their environment behaviorally and psychologically.

"Literature shows that there is a close relationship between IEQ and productivity," says Kim. "From this perspective, I would say measurement and verification of a building's on-site IEQ performance is the first step to ensure a productive work environment."

The "IEQ cart" includes instruments for testing several elements of the indoor environment.
Photo: Courtesy SmithGroupJJR

> *"The fact that people who work in the building daily report that Brock is performing well in terms of IEQ is a good indicator. We don't have to compromise comfort or productivity to design a net zero building."*

GREG MELLA
SmithGroupJJR

"In the Merrill Center, we moved from private office to an open environment. Over the years, we have learned to use our quiet voices, and we have also acclimated, so that we almost never get complaints about noise levels now. We'll use the information from this study to look at how we can work on the acoustics, and feel confident we'll get to the same place at the Brock Center. The lesson is, don't shy away from information. Use it to make a situation better."

MARY TOD WINCHESTER
Chesapeake Bay Foundation

Windows stay open as much as possible.
Photo: Prakash Patel

HEALTH

Imperative 08: CIVILIZED ENVIRONMENT
The Brock Center includes operable windows in every occupied space. Staff have learned to use these windows to optimize natural ventilation, and natural ventilation is being used more frequently than was anticipated.

Imperative 09: HEALTHY AIR
Ventilation strategies, including a Dedicated Outside Air System (DOAS), ensure adequate cycling of fresh air through the building.

Imperative 10: BIOPHILIA
The Brock Center incorporates all six biophilic design elements throughout the building.

MATERIALS

Imperative 11: RED LIST
All materials used in the Brock Center are Red List compliant or qualify for a relevant exemption under Living Building Challenge 2.1. In addition, the team sent advocacy letters to those manufacturers for which exemptions were required, urging them to replace Red List components and/or urging full disclosure of all ingredients. CBF continues to avoid Red List items when purchasing new materials or products for the Brock Center.

Imperative 12: CONSTRUCTION CARBON FOOTPRINT
To meet the requirements of this Imperative, CBF purchased 1,234 metric tonnes of carbon offsets through Sterling Planet to support a Landfill Gas to Energy project in Dartmouth, Massachusetts, thereby offsetting the carbon footprint of the carbon emissions produced during the construction of the Brock Center.

CBF staff are pleased with the Technion office furniture, which includes this conference room table and chairs. Photo: Dave Chance

Imperative 13: RESPONSIBLE INDUSTRY

All wood used in the Brock Center is either reclaimed or is FSC certified. The team went to great lengths to source and showcase reclaimed wood throughout the building. The team also sent advocacy letters to manufacturers, encouraging them to participate in relevant third-party certification programs.

Imperative 14: APPROPRIATE SOURCING

All materials used in the project meet the requirements of this Imperative.

Imperative 15: CONSERVATION AND REUSE

The project achieved the required recycling rates for construction debris. A conservation management plan has also been developed for every phase of the project, including design, construction, operation, and end of life.

CBF has implemented a vigorous recycling and composting program for staff and visitors. In addition, tours and educational programs include an environmental ethic, stressing the importance of resource conservation and waste reduction.

Chris Gorri reports that nearly all of the materials and products in the Brock Center are holding up extremely well. He and his staff are especially pleased with the Teknion office furniture, which in itself is a Living Building Challenge success story. CBF chose Teknion in part because of its commitment to transparency; the company also agreed to produce furniture for the Brock Center that is free of Red List ingredients, and to use FSC-certified wood. Teknion was so pleased with the results the changes were incorporated permanently. The company is also pursuing Declare labels for all of its products.

167

EQUITY

Imperative 16: HUMAN SCALE AND HUMANE PLACES

The Brock Center was designed on a scale that does not diminish either human visitors or the natural features that surround it. The building and the site provide a refuge from a built environment that can be noisy, crowded, and stressful. The building design promotes face-to-face interaction, and CBF's programs encourage community participation through its education programs and restoration activities.

Imperative 17: DEMOCRACY AND SOCIAL JUSTICE

The Brock Center was conceived as a gathering place for the community. People are welcome to visit the Center and enjoy access to Pleasure House Point, whether through CBF's programs or independently. The design of the building, along with entry ramps and ADA parking, ensure access for all. Interpretive and other signage complies with the Imperative's requirements.

Imperative 18: RIGHTS TO NATURE

The Brock Center does not contribute to air, water, noise, or light pollution, and it does not block entry to sunlight or public waterways; on the contrary, it provides access to shoreline habitats and the Lynnhaven River.

BEAUTY

Imperative 19: BEAUTY AND SPIRIT

Many aspects of the Brock Center celebrate culture, place, and spirit, and provide human delight. From the stories encapsulated in the salvaged materials to the pleasing curves of the building itself to the inspiring views enabled by the building's many windows, there are myriad ways people can find beauty in the Brock Center.

In early 2016, staff were given questionnaires about their experience working in a Living Building. The overwhelming majority of responses were positive. When prompted to name specific "delightful" features, respondents frequently mentioned the views, the abundance of natural light, the color palette, "natural" features such as the driftwood sculptures, and the south deck, which allows staff to work outside on nice days.

VOICES ON BEAUTY AND SPIRIT

"The Brock Center is the most peaceful place I have had the pleasure of working. Walking around the bend of the parking lot and seeing the curved structure of the building with the sun behind it gives me joy every morning."

"Merely being at Brock motivates and inspires one to engage more fully in the land and water that surround it and, subsequently, in the work of the CBF."

"I feel privileged and grateful to work in such a unique and inspiring space. The beauty and substance of the building and grounds draws so many people in, to learn more, and hopefully to create change."

Imperative 20: INSPIRATION AND EDUCATION

Education is the Brock Center's primary function. Regular tours expose thousands of people to the concepts of the Living Building Challenge through an inspiring case study. A dashboard in the lobby, also available online, provides real-time data on the building's water and energy use and energy production. Interpretive signage facilitates a richer understanding of The Chesapeake Bay ecosystem and the various features of the building.

In addition, CBF's boat- and land-based environmental education programs introduce thousands of children and adults to The Chesapeake Bay. Hands-on activities deepen their knowledge of the Bay's ecology and help them understand how their individual actions impact the Bay's water quality. Restoration programs offer another avenue through which volunteers can become actively invested in improving the health of the Bay.

ENERGY PERFORMANCE: LESSONS LEARNED

A Living Building is not a collection of static systems; rather, it responds to occupant behavior and changes in its operation. Since the Grand Opening, Greg Mella, and Building Operator Chris Gorri and his staff have collaborated to improve both the comfort and energy performance of the building.

The building management system (BMS), provided by Siemens, allows detailed daily monitoring of the Brock Center's performance. During the audit year, Mella requested that the daily energy report be emailed to him so he could monitor the building's performance. These reports divided energy use down to specific loads, such as lighting and pump energy. SmithGroupJJR compared the energy data against the energy use breakdown predicted by the energy model. As Mella discovered, it is possible to detect and even diagnose problems by observing patterns in different loads.

Photo: Dave Chance

169

"We found our energy model was pretty accurate," says Mella. "After a few months of comparison, we could see right away when Brock was operating in a manner different from what was predicted, ultimately indicating that there was a malfunction somewhere."

CBF staff were also invested in meeting the net zero energy goal, and were willing to conserve energy whenever possible. Once CBF personnel grew comfortable with its baseline energy consumption, they began to expand building usage to include weekend and evening events. As Gorri and staff learned about the new building, Gorri also made adjustments to the building management system. Staff also learned which windows to open and close to optimize natural ventilation.

LIGHTING

- The impressive reductions in the lighting load are attributable in large part to a design that enhances daylighting. Very little light is needed in the building, even on gray or rainy days. CBF's decision to turn off, rather than dim, most lighting during the day also had a large impact on reducing this load.

- Individual task lights are a good energy-saving solution for staff who work late. Each desk at the Brock Center is fitted with a LED task light equipped with an occupancy sensor.

- Glare is only an issue during the winter months, when the sun is the lowest in the morning. Sun shades are used to prevent glare on staff desks during those months.

- The interior lighting system is highly efficient, but more complex than necessary. A programmer must be brought in from out of state to make any major changes. A simple system with occupancy sensors and wall switches would have been adequate.

PLUG LOADS

- The "master" vampire switch effectively saves energy by cutting power to most of the plugs in the building after hours. The switch also serves as an effective teaching tool for visitors. Taking note of occupant behavior and patterns, Chris Gorri adjusted the timing of the vampire switch to better match staff's schedules.

- A copy machine was found to be an "energy hog," even though it was ENERGY STAR certified. CBF replaced the machine with a more efficient unit.

CONDITIONING ENERGY AND NATURAL VENTILATION

- The combination of a super-efficient envelope, an efficient VRF system that relies on earth-modulated water, and the extensive use of natural ventilation resulted in a 67 percent reduction in heating and cooling energy compared to a typical building.

- Chris Gorri learned that the building is easier to keep cool than it is to heat, in part because staff prefer warmer temperatures. Over the course of the year, he adjusted the heating and cooling set points, a task made easy with the Building Management System. Gorri has also noticed that perception influences comfort. For example, staff feel colder on gray days compared to sunny days, even if the inside temperature is the same.

- Ceiling fans allow CBF to push the limits on natural ventilation, saving cooling energy. Staff have also discovered when to open windows strategically to maximize thermal comfort, and enjoy participating in the day-to-day functional performance of the building.

- Night flushing cools the building after hours. If preset temperature and humidity conditions are met, the upper clerestory windows automatically open to provide natural ventilation when the building is unoccupied. These windows can also be "told" to open during occupied hours.

ACTUAL ENERGY CONSUMPTION:
AVERAGE BUILDING

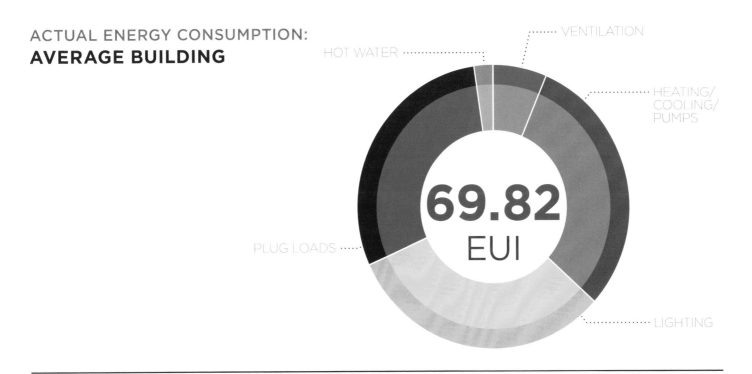

HOT WATER

VENTILATION

HEATING/
COOLING/
PUMPS

69.82
EUI

PLUG LOADS

LIGHTING

ACTUAL ENERGY CONSUMPTION:
BROCK ENVIRONMENTAL CENTER

VENTILATION SAVINGS
- natural ventilation
- dedicated outside air system

HEATING/COOLING SAVINGS
- ground source exchange
- efficient HVAC system
- high performance envelope
- natural ventilation
- exterior shading

LIGHTING SAVINGS
- daylighting and controls

PLUG LOAD SAVINGS
- energy star equipment
- plug load controls

HOT WATER SAVINGS
- water conservation

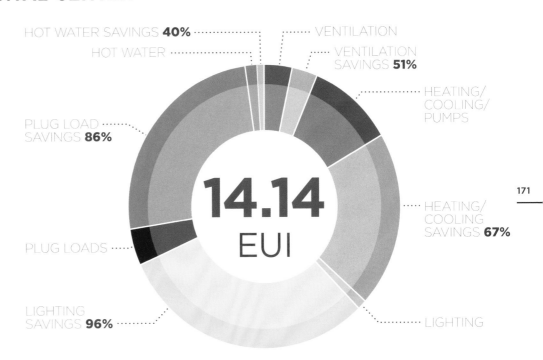

HOT WATER SAVINGS **40%**

HOT WATER

VENTILATION

VENTILATION
SAVINGS **51%**

PLUG LOAD
SAVINGS **86%**

HEATING/
COOLING/
PUMPS

14.14
EUI

PLUG LOADS

HEATING/
COOLING
SAVINGS **67%**

LIGHTING
SAVINGS **96%**

LIGHTING

WIND POWER: LESSONS LEARNED

The pair of Bergey wind turbines bookending the Brock Environmental Center are visible symbols of CBF's commitment to renewable energy. They are also a viable source of clean energy for this windy coastal site. For project teams considering adding wind power to the mix of renewable energy sources, the Brock team offers some valuable lessons about cost and performance:

- CBF has found that the turbines require little to no maintenance and are quiet except during extremely strong winds, when the turbine inverter shuts off and begins to freewheel. CBF worked with the manufacturer to raise the "set point" speed at which the turbine inverter shuts off, as this was happening too frequently.

- Wind speeds are difficult to predict and often vary from historic averages. In addition, wind is greatly impacted by terrain. Consequently, two sites that are very close to each other might experience very different wind speeds.

- A site's soil characteristic impacts cost. The Brock Center's sandy site required piles to be driven 110 feet below the ground to support the turbines—a feature which drove up the cost significantly.

- Single storms can have a dramatic impact on wind production. For example, in early October, Hurricane Joaquin caused sustained high wind speeds for five days, creating a large spike in production.

- CBF continues to field questions about the potential for wind turbines to kill birds. Along with advocating for wind power, CBF wanted to be transparent about any negative impacts. Since the turbines were commissioned, CBF staff have been monitoring the area for bird kills. Since June of 2014, CBF has found six dead gulls near the turbines. Four of these deaths occurred during periods of exceptionally high winds.

- Finally, the wind turbines provide excellent learning opportunities and even serve as ambassadors for the Brock Center. Whereas the building itself is low in profile and tucked away on the site, the sculptural turbines are more visible, drawing curious visitors to the center.

172

The Brock Center is proving that small-scale wind turbines are a viable strategy for certain locations.
Photo: Chris Gorri

"Most of the time architects and builders design and build the project, then hand over the key and they're gone. You never really know how what you designed actually performs—you get this disconnect. The Living Building Challenge creates a condition which allows architects and builders to engage in the project during the performance period. It's a really transformational thing in terms of informing our practices as designers and builders."

ELIZABETH HEIDER
Skanska USA

FANS AND PUMPS

- The energy required to operate fans for the ventilation system was higher than predicted. SmithGroupJJR's energy model underestimated actual fan energy, in part because the model assumed the VRF units would be able to turn the indoor fans off whenever space temperature for that zone was satisfied; however, fans in the wall-mounted VRF units are programmed to run anytime the system is enabled. These controls cannot be overridden by the BMS or altered at the factory.

- Pump energy was also higher than predicted, especially during the heating season near the end of the reporting year. Mella and Coffield do not know exactly why this is, but have offered several possible explanations, including mistakes in the energy model and a possible pump malfunction.

- Detecting anomalies in pump loads helped CBF detect a problem with a pump that was running continuously following several power outages.

173

LIVING BUILDING PARTNERS

OWNER
Chesapeake Bay Foundation

ARCHITECT
SmithGroupJJR

MEP/FP ENGINEER
SmithGroupJJR

PROJECT MANAGEMENT
Skanska USA

CONTRACTOR
Hourigan Construction

DESIGN ADVISORY GROUP
Jason F. McLennan, Russell Perry,
Elizabeth Heider, and Rob Watson

**LEED/LIVING BUILDING
CHALLENGE CONSULTANT**
Janet Harrison, Architect

**COMMISSIONING AGENT
(MEP SYSTEMS)**
Wright Commissioning

**BUILDING ENCLOSURE
COMMISSIONING AGENT**
The Façade Group

**AUTHORITY HAVING
JURISDICTION**
City of Virginia Beach

**SITE DESIGN/
CIVIL ENGINEERING**
WPL Site Design

STRUCTURAL ENGINEERING
A&F Engineers

**GEOTECHNICAL
CONSULTANT**
Engineering and Testing Services
(ETS)

ENERGY MODELING
Baumann Consulting

**WATERWORKS
DESIGN CONSULTING**
Biohabitats

**WATERWORKS
OPERATOR**
MSA, P.C.

AWARDS AND HONORS

2017

AIA COMMITTEE ON THE ENVIRONMENT (COTE)

COTE Top Ten Plus Award

2016

SUSTAINABLE BUILDINGS INDUSTRY COUNCIL/ BEYOND GREEN

High Performance Building & Community Award

BUILDING INTELLIGENCE GROUP

Sustainability Initiative of the Year

THE CHICAGO ATHENAEUM MUSEUM OF ARCHITECTURE AND DESIGN

Green Good Design Award

AMERICAN SOCIETY OF HEATING, REFRIGERATING AND AIR-CONDITIONING ENGINEERS (ASHRAE)

National Technology Award, Second Place, Commercial Buildings - New

AIA MARYLAND

Honor Award - Institutional Architecture

ENGINEERING NEWS RECORD (ENR)

Best of the Best Green Project

AMERICAN SOCIETY OF LANDSCAPE ARCHITECTURE (ASLA)

Technology Award - Second Place, Category I - New Commercial Buildings

ASCE ARCHITECTURAL ENGINEERING INSTITUTE (AEI)

Award of Excellence - Mechanical Systems Design

ASCE ARCHITECTURAL ENGINEERING INSTITUTE (AEI)

Award of Merit - Architectural Engineering Integration

ASCE ARCHITECTURAL ENGINEERING INSTITUTE (AEI)

Award of Merit - Electrical Systems Design

AIA NORTHERN VIRGINIA

Award of Excellence - Commercial Architecture

WAN SUSTAINABLE BUILDINGS AWARD

Shortlist

2015

AMERICAN SOCIETY OF HEATING, REFRIGERATING AND AIR-CONDITIONING ENGINEERS (ASHRAE)

Regional Technology Award - Commercial Projects

AMERICAN SOCIETY OF HEATING, REFRIGERATING AND AIR-CONDITIONING ENGINEERS (ASHRAE)

Local Technology Award - Commercial Projects

VIRGINIA DEPARTMENT OF ENVIRONMENTAL QUALITY

Governor's Environmental Excellence Award (Virginia)

AMERICAN PLANNING ASSOCIATION (APA) SUSTAINABLE DIVISION

Sustainable Urban Design or Preservation Plan or Project Award

ENR MID-ATLANTIC

Best Green Project

HAMPTON ROADS ASSOCIATION FOR COMMERCIAL REAL ESTATE

Best Master Planned Project - Award of Excellence

HAMPTON ROADS ASSOCIATION FOR COMMERCIAL REAL ESTATE

Best Sustainable Design - Award of Excellence

HAMPTON ROADS ASSOCIATION FOR COMMERCIAL REAL ESTATE

Juror's Choice Award - Excellence in Development Design

AMERICAN PLANNING ASSOCIATION

Sustainable Building Project Award

ASSOCIATED BUILDERS AND CONTRACTORS

Award of Excellence, Best Institutional Building

ASSOCIATED BUILDERS AND CONTRACTORS

Overall Excellence in Construction Award

ENR MID-ATLANTIC

Best Overall Safety Project

INTERNATIONAL
LIVING FUTURE INSTITUTE

The International Living Future Institute is an environmental
NGO committed to catalyzing the transformation toward
communities that are socially just, culturally rich, and ecologically
restorative. The Institute is premised on the belief that providing
a compelling vision for the future is a fundamental requirement
for reconciling humanity's relationship with the natural world.
The Institute operates the Living Building Challenge, the
built environment's most rigorous performance standard, and
Declare, an ingredients label for building materials. It houses
the Cascadia Green Building Council and Ecotone Publishing.

ECOTONE PUBLISHING

Founded by green building experts in 2004, Ecotone Publishing
is dedicated to meeting the growing demand for authoritative
and accessible books on sustainable design, materials selection
and building techniques in North America and beyond. Located
in the Cascadia region, Ecotone is well positioned to play
an important part in the green design movement. Ecotone
searches out and documents inspiring projects, visionary
people, and vital trends that are leading the design industry
to transformational change toward a healthier planet.

LIVING BUILDING CHALLENGE

The Living Building Challenge is the built environment's most
rigorous performance standard. It calls for the creation of
building projects at all scales that operate as cleanly, beautifully,
and efficiently as nature's architecture. To be certified under the
Challenge, projects must meet a series of ambitious performance
requirements, including net zero energy, waste and water,
over a minimum of 12 months of continuous occupancy.